Egermeier's
Stories of Great Men and Women

Stories for Boys and Girls

By Elsie E. Egermeier

Revision by Zelpha H. Anderson

Illustrations by Bernard Case

THE WARNER PRESS • ANDERSON, INDIANA

CONTENTS

Chapter 1

SUSAN B. ANTHONY

She Opened Doors for Women

AMONG the Berkshire Hills, near the sleepy little village of Adams, Massachusetts, one cold day in February, 1820, Susan Brownell, the second daughter of Daniel and Lucy Anthony, was born. There for six years she lived to enjoy the wealth of scenery which surrounds her birthplace. She spent a happy childhood with her little sisters, Guelma and Hannah, and their baby brother, Daniel, for playmates.

From those early days Susan cherished the memory of visits to the homes of her grandparents, who lived near by. The children passed Grandmother Read's home each day on their way to and from school. Susan and Guelma were always in a hurry to start early for school, not because they wished to be the first to arrive at the schoolroom, but because they knew that if they started in plenty of time they might stop for a few minutes at

Grandmother's house. She would be sure to give them a taste of her fresh cheesecurd and a sip of her homemade "coffee." In spite of their good, warm breakfast at home, these little girls seemed to think that a lunch at Grandmother's house tasted better than anything else.

And no less attractive was Grandmother Anthony's house. There in the closet beneath the parlor stairs the tub containing maple sugar was kept, and the children had free access to it. When they started for home they sometimes carried such goodies as apples or doughnuts or caraway cakes.

Then one day the big green wagon with the two fine horses came all the way from Battenville, New York, to carry them off to a new home. It was no wonder that the little girls were teary-eyed when they climbed aboard with their mother and baby Daniel. Their grandmothers, teary-eyed too, were being left behind!

With a loving mother and a kind, sympathetic father, the children soon found that their home life continued the same as before, though in the midst of strange surroundings. At first they were frightened to see dark-skinned men and women who were slaves of some of the people in the village. There had been no slaves near their childhood home in Massachusetts, and they had never seen Negroes before.

Susan's father was a cotton manufacturer and a merchant. Because he had grown so successful in Adams, Massachusetts, he had been invited to come to Battenville, New York, and do a bigger business as a manufacturer and merchant. When first he set up business there his partner was disappointed to learn that he refused to sell liquor in his store.

"The farmers will not trade here if you refuse to furnish liquor for them," said his partner.

"Then they will have to trade elsewhere," replied Susan's father.

He stocked his shelves with the best goods and advertised them at the lowest prices. When the farmers learned that he was honest and believed in square dealing, they gladly patronized his store. In the factory, the sawmill, and the gristmill, he refused to employ workers who drank to excess, and he organized a temperance society in the town. Susan learned from her father's attitude that intemperance is one of the greatest evils people face.

As the Anthony girls grew older, sometimes they were permitted to visit the factory. They spent hours watching the employees at work. By and by they felt certain that they could do the work quite as well as the regular workers. Then one day an employee became ill and there was no one to take her place at the "spooler." Susan and her younger sister Hannah were both eager to act as a substitute until the girl recovered. Their father, who believed that all honest toil is good, consented to let them draw straws and decide in that way which one should go. "The winner," said he, "must be willing to divide her earnings with the loser, for both of you want to do the work."

Susan drew the lucky straw, and so she spent two weeks as a factory worker, operating the "spooler." Her wages for this time amounted to three dollars, and according to their agreement she gave half the amount to her sister. Then instead of spending what was left of her earnings on herself, she bought half a dozen pale blue cups and saucers which her mother had admired in the store and gave them to her.

Susan's mother was a very busy woman. Her family now consisted of six children, and she boarded nearly a dozen brickmakers and factory hands. She taught her young daughters how to become neat housekeepers and good cooks. Once when Susan

7

was only twelve years old Mrs. Anthony became ill. During her illness the three girls did the housework and packed lunches in the dinner pails of the workmen just as carefully as their mother had done.

In Battenville was an old-fashioned school taught in winter by a man and in summer by a woman. Schoolteachers received so little pay for their services that free school education was not given much consideration. The Anthony children attended the public school when they first came to the village, and Susan advanced rapidly in her studies. When she was ready to begin long division her teacher refused to enroll her in the class. "Girls do not need to know so much about mathematics," he said. Susan did not agree with him. She felt unhappy because she was being refused the privilege of studying whatever she preferred, just because she happened to be a girl.

Her father, hearing of the difficulty, felt sorry for Susan. He wanted his children to learn all they could from books, and he saw that the instructors in the village school could not teach them all they might wish to learn. Then he furnished a large room in his new brick store for a schoolroom and hired a teacher to instruct his children. There no special favor was shown to boy students, and Susan was happy.

Susan always found her father an understanding friend. He consented when she wanted to teach summer school at the age of fifteen. Some people criticized him for allowing her to work, because he was wealthy. But he believed that all young people should be encouraged to become self-supporting, and he allowed his daughters, as well as his sons, to choose their occupations. As a teacher Susan received only a dollar a week and her board, but she felt that she was doing something worth while in the world. Two years later she taught a winter term of school and received $1.50 a week, boarding around in the homes of her pupils. The next year she went with her sister Guelma to a boarding school near Philadelphia.

Unhappy hours now came to Susan, for she had never been so far from home before. Her teacher, a grave Quaker woman, did not understand the natural longings of a young girl for wholesome fun. Often she criticized Susan severely. One day, Susan saw cobwebs hanging from the ceiling, and cobwebs, she had been taught, are quite out of place in a tidy room. Trying to please her teacher, she found a broom at recess and began brushing them down. Some which she could not reach were hanging above the teacher's desk. So she climbed up on the desk and was poking the broom around vigorously when "snap!" went a hinge, and the desk broke beneath her weight. Instead of thanks, she received a severe scolding. Her teacher seemed to dislike her even more than before.

In spite of these unpleasant happenings Susan kept bravely on with her studies. She longed to learn everything that books could teach her. Like some other girls in that time, she was much displeased because girl students were not admitted to colleges. She longed to make the best of educational opportunities offered by the boarding school, even thought her teacher seemed unreasonable.

Her father's failure in business prevented Susan from continuing her studies at the boarding school longer than one year. She returned home in time to see everything, even her mother's silver wedding spoons, collected to be sold in order to pay off her father's debt.

"This is not fair," cried Susan indignantly. "Why should Mother's things be sold to pay off Father's debt? Has she no right to her own possessions?"

"The law demands it," was the answer she received.

"Then," declared Susan, "the law ought to be changed."

9

Susan now began to teach school in earnest, for she wished to earn all she could to help the family. Yet, although she was a capable teacher, she received only one fourth as much salary as was being paid to men who taught school. Again Susan felt indignant. "It is not right," said she, "that women whose work is just as good or better than men's should receive only one fourth as much wages." From that time she began to think much about the unfairness done to women. And she determined to correct this wrong.

All her lifetime Susan had been a wide-awake, intelligent girl, taking an interest in everything about her which concerned the welfare of people. She shared her father's sympathy for the slaves who worked in the cotton fields of the South and was glad when President Lincoln proclaimed their freedom. She also shared her father's conviction that intemperance is a great evil, and while teaching school she was asked to make her first public address in a temperance meeting.

She knew that other thoughtful people were becoming stirred to fight against these wrongs too, but few seemed to be awakening to the needs of more consideration for women. Susan felt that women were not granted as much right as the freed slaves. There was no law of the state or of the nation to offer protection to a drunkard's wife, however cruelly he might treat her. Married women, she learned, had no property rights at all, according to law. "Something must be done about this," declared Susan emphatically.

When the People's College was about to be founded at Seneca Falls, New York, Susan remembered how earnestly she had longed to share college privileges with her brothers. She knew other girls desired a good education just as much as she did, and she went to that city to urge the admission of girl students into the new college. While there she met other women who felt as troubled as she did about the unfair laws of the country. With them she began the great work of her lifetime, trying to change those laws and obtain for womankind their full rights as citizens of the United States of America.

Susan's task proved to be more difficult than she realized, for it is never easy to change long-established customs. However, she was a brave girl, not afraid to protest against what she believed to be wrong. The mere fact that wrong customs had prevailed for ages did not make them any less wrong. She believed that the time had come for people to see the matter as she did. Now she gave up her work of teaching school and began to travel from city to city, lecturing on the need of woman's rights. She spoke in crowded halls, in churches, or wherever she was given an audience, and by and by she became one of the noted speakers of the century. Her lecture tours sometimes kept her away from home for months at a time, and she traveled from coast to coast.

Though she did not see results at once, Susan did not give up in discouragement. She drafted the Federal Suffrage Amendment, which gives women the privilege to vote, nearly fifty years before that amendment became a part of the Constitution of the United States. But her untiring efforts helped to correct the inconsideration shown to women. She lived to see the time when College doors swung open to girls as well as to boys, when married women's property rights were considered, and when women wage earners were no longer regarded as unworthy to receive as much for their services as men. Before the close of her life, girls might fit themselves to become doctors, lawyers, businesswomen, or anything they chose to be. This was quite a contrast to conditions which ambitious girls met when Susan was born. At that time only the three occupations of servant, factory worker, and teacher were open to them, and none paid more than the barest living wage.

Susan B. Anthony was one of the greatest friends the women of the United States of America ever had. During her lifetime she was often misunderstood. Many unkind things were said about her, and she suffered rude treatment. But always she kept on trying to do what she believed to be right and bravely letting others know about her convictions.

Chapter 2

CLARA BARTON

She Forgot to Be Afraid

A CHRISTMAS baby at the Bartons"—this was the news which spread through a New England neighborhood in the winter of 1821, when little Clara was born. The Bartons were farmers, living several miles from Oxford, Massachusetts, and their family of boys and girls were nearly all grown up when the baby sister was born. No one realized that the new member of the household would someday grow up to become one of the most famous women of her country.

Because she had no playmates in her early childhood, little Clara often watched others at their work and learned from them how to do simple tasks. She found more joy in helping others by running errands and doing little chores than in playing alone. Always she would hurry back and ask more questions, hoping to find something else to do.

When the weather was warm and sunny Clara enjoyed being out of doors. The one person she liked best of all to follow about his work was her big brother David. He was seldom too busy to take her along with him, and sometimes he allowed her to help him drop potatoes down the long rows, or hold the lines as they drove the wagon across the fields. He would take her with him on horseback when he rode to the pasture after the cows. He would try to answer her funny little questions in a kind, big-brotherly way.

Clara was such an eager little helper that David taught her how to do many things. He taught her how to drive a nail straight, how to tie a knot that would hold, and one evening he taught her how to milk a cow. Clara felt happy when he praised her for learning so quickly everything he tried to teach. One day he placed her in the saddle all alone and taught her how to ride a horse.

Clara enjoyed being out of doors, and quickly learned how to ride horseback so well that she could bring the cows from pasture alone and carry messages across the field in a hurry. No one would have guessed, to see the little five-year-old girl dash away on the most spirited pony in her father's pasture, that she knew the meaning of fear.

But at heart little Clara was timid and afraid. The world seemed so great and mysterious, and the people seemed so hard to understand. When strangers came on the place she shrank out of sight, for she felt afraid of them. Then there were the awful thunderstorms in summer; how she trembled as the crashing noises came! Sometimes, strange as it may seem, Clara felt afraid of herself, for there were no other little children near with whom she could romp and play and whose feelings she could understand. The little girl who often raced across the

New England hills on her fleet-footed pony was not always happy.

Clara's father had been a soldier in the Revolutionary War. When his baby girl grew old enough to beg for "more stories, Papa," he would take her on his knee and tell her about the time when he went out to fight against the enemy and help gain independence for his country. He would tell about his daring leader, Mad Anthony Wayne, who led him into many a battle. He would tell of the clouds of black smoke which rose over the battlefields, and of how the hills and woodlands re-echoed with the report of their flintlock guns. Then the birds would leave their nests in fright, and the furry woodland folk would rush pell-mell, here and there, trying to find places of safety. Little Clara would listen with solemn eyes, and then she would ask, "What happened to the men who got shot, Papa?" And he would shake his head sadly and reply, "Alas, my little daughter, I cannot tell; for we had to leave them while we chased the Redcoats away from our beloved land." Clara would shudder as she cuddled up closer in her father's strong arms, for she would think about the suffering men who had no one to wash their wounds, no one to bring them a drink of cool water, and no one to comfort them in their dying hour.

Two miles up the road from the Barton home stood a country schoolhouse. There Clara learned how to overcome some of her shyness. Both summer and winter terms of school she attended, while the wonders of the book world began to unfold before her eager mind. Then she studied for a while at home, with her teacher brother for instructor. She learned her lessons well, and she also came to understand how children think and feel. This helped her to be kind and patient with other children when she became a school teacher herself.

When Clara was eleven years old, her big brother David fell

from a tall building and injured himself. The men with whom he was working carried him home, and there he was placed in a clean, white bed to get well. But instead of getting well he grew worse, and for two years he was an invalid. Clara remembered the kind things he used to do for her when she was a tiny girl following him about the place, and now she became his nurse. Day after day she smoothed his pillow, brought him cool water from the well when he was thirsty. She entertained him by reading stories from her schoolbooks or by telling him the happenings about the farm. She willingly denied herself the pleasure of many horseback rides just to stay in his room and try to make him comfortable.

After David recovered, Clara decided to become a schoolteacher. She studied harder than ever and learned everything that was taught in the country schoolhouse. Then, although still a very young girl, she lengthened her dresses, wound her hair in neat coils about her head, and pretended to be quite grown up, for she wished to teach the neighborhood school. "We will let her try," agreed the members of the school board, although they knew she was not yet sixteen years old. And Clara succeeded, for she won the love of the children and the respect of the big, rude boys who used to make trouble in the schoolroom. They found out that she was not cross or unreasonable, but that she had the courage to demand of them an honest effort to learn. Soon they quit trying to provoke her, for they liked her frank, earnest manner and were glad to treat her as a friend.

Clara saved her small earnings until she had enough money to pay her way through a school in Clinton, New York. After graduating from that school she went still farther from home to open a free school for girls and boys in Bordentown, New Jersey. She began teaching there in a tumble-down building with only six pupils. "Everyone is welcome, rich or poor," she said, and after a few weeks passed she had more pupils than the room would hold. At the end of the year a free school building was erected, and five hundred children enrolled to attend the first term. Clara was asked to be the principal of the school, and she continued to teach there for a number of years. Perhaps she thought she would teach school all the rest of her lifetime, for she loved children and understood how to encourage them to do well.

Clara could do other things just as well as she could teach in a schoolroom. She understood business and could straighten out tangles in figures as well as fights on the school playground. When she went to Washington, D.C., to visit relatives and take a rest from teaching, she was asked to help straighten out some tangles in the Patent Office. All the other clerks were men, and they were displeased when she came to work among them. They feared she would discover the mistakes they had made. They were rude and poked fun at her, hoping that such treatment would soon cause her to quit. Clara paid no attention to their unkind actions and went on with her duties. Soon she traced the tangles back to the clerks' mistakes, and they were dismissed. She was asked to continue as a worker in the Patent Office.

While Clara was at work there the great Civil War broke out. Soon the roar of cannons could be heard, and black clouds of smoke could be seen rising above the battlefields near Washington. Clara remembered the stories her father used to tell about his soldier life. She remembered, too, the sadness which would steal into her heart when she thought of the wounded men who died without anyone to comfort them on the bloody battlegrounds. Now she knew this same horrible thing was happening again, and she felt a great longing to help the wounded men.

At her first opportunity Clara visited an army hospital, where doctors and nurses were caring for the sufferers who were brought in from the battlefield. Some of them had been left so long that they were nearly dead when at last they reached the hospital. Clara felt that they had suffered needlessly, and she decided that help should be sent to other wounded men on the battlefields themselves just as soon as the smoke would clear away enough for wounded men to be found. Because the doctors and nurses were unwilling to go nearer the danger line than the army hospitals, Clara had to be content for a while with taking provisions in a boat up the Potomac River to the sufferers and bringing back as many of the wounded as the boat could carry. Only a few could be relieved in this way, but as long as the fighting continued along the shores of the Potomac she bravely rowed her boat across the water and back again, risking the fire from the guns.

After a while the battle front drew away from the river. Then Clara begged permission to follow the cannons and be ready to help as soon as the fight would end. Her aged father had encouraged her to attempt this great work, and with tears in her eyes she pleaded for the privilege, saying, "My father was a soldier. He told me how much it would mean, and told me of the dangers." Finally, contrary to army regulations, she was allowed to take a supply of bandages and other necessities and pitch her tent with the regular army drawn up for battle.

On these bloody fields Clara began her great lifework. Although a timid little woman, she forgot her own fears in her eagerness to relieve the sufferings of others. She bound up ugly wounds, bathed fevered brows, and cooled parched lips from her own canteen. Day after day she worked, and often far into the night. Sometimes she traveled on horseback, sometimes in an army wagon. But on and on she went, keeping at the battle front with her first aid to the wounded.

Once when no food supplies had been sent, Clara found that the medicine bottles had been packed in fine meal; so she borrowed several big kettles from a farmhouse and cooked the meal to serve to her half-starved patients until other supplies reached them. She did not hesitate to go with her own throat parched and her face blackened by sulphurous smoke to answer the groans of a dying soldier. She ministered to all alike, whatever uniform they wore, for she sympathized with anyone who was suffering, not just with the men who fought in the cause which she believed to be right. No wonder she was called the "Angel of the Battlefield."

Although Clara risked her life on sixteen battlefields during the Civil War, not once was she injured. Often her clothing was torn by shells. Once when she stooped to lift the head of a wounded soldier a bullet whizzed between her arm and her body, instantly killing the man.

After the War ended, Clara spent several years helping to trace missing soldiers. Many letters came to her from mothers whose sons had been killed and who wished to learn where their bodies were buried. She also returned to mothers and wives and sweethearts many keepsakes which had been left with her by dying men.

When at last this sad task was finished, Clara was worn out. She went to Europe to rest and to try to forget the misery she had seen. There again she was called by the cruel demands of war to bind up more wounds and comfort other sufferers in the Franco-Prussian war. Clara found that there were Red Cross societies in Europe to whom permission was given to care for the wounded and dying on any battlefield. She was pleased with the good work of this society and wished that her own people in America would organize such a society, too.

Clara returned to America full of enthusiasm to organize a Red Cross society in her native land. She talked to everyone whom she met about the wonderful work which the Red Cross accomplished in Europe. To her great surprise and disappointment, few people seemed interested.

"We shall never have another war," many told her when she talked about the benefits of such a society.

"But we may have disasters," she would reply, "and people who suffer from flood, or from famine, or earthquake, or from any other calamity are just as needy and deserving of our organized interest and ready relief as are soldiers on a battlefield."

After years of waiting and working, Clara finally convinced the people that an American Red Cross society would be a worthy organization. She was chosen to serve as its first president and remained in that office until she was an old woman, retiring at the age of eighty-three years. She lived on at her Red Cross home in Glen Echo, Maryland, until her death on April 12, 1912. This was just two years before the first world war, a struggle which called for the best efforts of all Red Cross societies to minister to the needs of suffering people in many lands.

Chapter 3

ALEXANDER GRAHAM BELL

He Discovered that Wire Can Talk

WHEN the telephone was first invented, people wagged their heads. "That newfangled thing will never amount to much," they said. "It is only a toy." But years have passed. Great continents are crossed by wires that make it possible for the human voice to be heard and clearly understood thousands of miles away.

Because the telephone has come to fill such an important part in the daily business and social life of the world, humanity owes a debt of gratitude to its inventor. To Alexander Graham Bell belongs the credit for the invention of the telephone. As a tribute to him a great telephone system which covers the United States bears his name—the Bell Telephone Company.

Twenty-nine years before the origin of the telephone in the United States, Alexander Graham Bell was born in the city of Edinburgh, Scotland, on March 3, 1847. His father was a lecturer on elocution in the University of Edinburgh, and for a long time had been interested in the science of sound. An uncle and grandfather had also specialized in the study of the laws of speech and sound and had taught and written on that subject. Doubtless little Alexander and his two brothers often heard them discuss their work. As they grew older these boys came to know about the system of "visible speech" which their father and grandfather had worked out for use in teaching correct speaking. This system, using symbols based on the form and action of the vocal organs, enabled persons who had been born deaf to learn to talk. The Bell brothers soon discovered that their father's work was fascinating, and all three of them grew up to specialize in the same line of study.

Alexander attended school in Edinburgh, and at the age of fourteen he graduated from the Royal High School of that city. He also studied music, his mother being his instructor at the piano. From his study of music, he added to his knowledge of the science of sound.

Alexander was very much an ordinary boy, as fond of fun as any boy. Sometimes he went out into the country to play near a gristmill with the son of the miller. What fun they had scampering about on the banks of the millstream! One day the miller said, "Boys, I think you are growing old enough to learn how to do useful work."

"What can we do?" asked Alexander.

"You might help me remove the husks from this wheat," answered the busy man.

The two boys set to work at what proved to be quite a hard task. Their fingers were not used to such work, and the husks wore at the tender flesh. Alexander wondered whether there would not be an easier way to remove the husks. "Why not use a small brush? he reasoned. He found one and tried it. Sure enough, the husks came off easier and he could do two or three times as much work.

"So far, so good," thought young Alexander. "Why not put this wheat into the large rotary tank that is used in the mill, and let the paddle wheel throw it against brushes, or something rough like a brush?"

He spoke to the miller about this plan, and the miller was pleased with the idea. They tried the experiment and found that it worked well. This was Alexander's first experiment—an invention that helped people.

Alexander had no notion of becoming a miller when he would grow up. Like all boys who greatly admire their fathers, he planned to follow his father's profession. As a little boy he used to play that he was a professor. One time he organized his friends into a club which they called "The Society for the Promotion of Fine Arts Among Boys." In this society every member could be a professor, and Alexander styled himself Professor of Anatomy. He set about to make a collection of skeletons, animals, and birds. His father encouraged him by giving suggestions and even by helping him collect objects for study.

One time the young "professor" arranged to give a lecture on anatomy to a group of equally ambitious boys. He brought a dead little pig to dissect, and when he thrust a knife into the carcass, a groaning sound came from its depths, caused by the sudden escape of some air that had remained in the animal. This unexpected sound threw the "professor" in a panic, and the last seen of him on that occasion was when he made a frightened exit through the door. Thereafter his interest in the society lost its fervor and he turned his attention to other things.

Young Alexander carried on his experiments at home as well as when in company with his boy friends. He undertook the task of teaching his pet dog how to talk. Patiently he kept at it until he found out that by manipulating the dog's lower jaw the animal would make a noise that sounded like "Ow-ah-oo, ga-ma-ma." This, according to Alexander's interpretation meant, "How are you, Grandmama?" Great was his delight when entertaining his friends to demonstrate before them this ability of his dog to talk.

After graduating from the Edinburgh high school Alexander spent a year in London with his grandfather. While there he became more interested than ever in the science of sound, and studied it very seriously. His brothers were also specializing in this study and were preparing to teach. Before he was seventeen years old he, too, applied for a position as teacher in an academy at Elgin, Scotland, and was accepted. There his salary was fifty dollars a year and board, with instruction in Latin and Greek to fit him for the University. He must have proved himself a capable teacher student, for later he enrolled at the Edinburgh University. In due time he completed his work there and returned to Elgin Academy to become master and teacher of elocution and music.

Not long after this the Bell family left their home in Scotland and moved to London. Since Alexander wished to continue his studies, he joined the family in London and enrolled at the University College and later at London University. During these years he became deeply interested in the teaching of deaf-born children, and before he was twenty-one he had taught many of them to speak. Because of this success he was chosen to carry on his father's work when the elder Bell left England for a lecture tour in America.

Another experiment now began to interest Alexander. He found that by using an electromagnet he could produce vibrations on a tuning fork which might lead him into scientific discovery. However, he was hindered from carrying on this experiment by illness which threatened his life.

Alexander's two brothers had died from tuberculosis, and now it seemed that he would develop the same disease. His parents decided to take him to another climate, hoping that the change would restore his health. Once more they packed their belongings and sailed to America. Here they lived near Brantford, Ontario, Canada, and in a short time Alexander's health began to improve.

Near their new home lived a tribe of Mohawk Indians—the first red men of Alexander's acquaintance. He spent much time visiting them and teaching them the sign language called "visible speech," which his father had invented. Soon after the Board of Education of Boston heard of his work they invited him to come to their city and teach in a school for deaf-mutes. Through his success in that school he won a professorship in Boston University.

Now Alexander's interest began to broaden and include the mysteries of telegraphy. He knew that telegraph messages are carried by means of a charged wire, and he wondered why the human voice could not be carried on the wire. The more he thought about this idea the more reasonable it seemed to him, and he began to try to make an instrument that would send the voice over the wire and catch its clear tones at the other end.

Alexander realized that he could not make such an instrument by himself. He needed a helper who believed that the thing could be done. He needed someone who knew how to build all sorts of apparatus that inventors need. He found just such a man in his young friend, Thomas Watson. Thomas was doing the kind of work Alexander's helper would have to know how to do. Alexander told him about the new invention which he believed he could bring about with someone's help.

At first Thomas was too much surprised at the thought of such a new invention to know how to answer his friend. But he finally agreed to help Alexander, and the two young men set to work. They strung a wire through the house in which they were rooming and at each end they attached a small instrument which Alexander had instructed Thomas to make. Then Thomas took his station in the basement, down three flights of stairs, and Alexander tried to talk to him. A sound came over the wire which Thomas recognized as Alexander's voice, but he could not make out a word. This did not discourage the young men, for they knew they were on the right track. They continued to work and work, trying to improve the instrument.

Months passed by, and nearly a year, and then one day while trying out their latest improvement Thomas heard Alexander say, "Watson, come here. I want you." With a bound of delight Thomas sprang up the flight of stairs, and Alexander met him with a beaming face. At last they had succeeded.

So sure had they been of success that several weeks before this happened young Bell had applied to the patent office in Washington D.C., for a patent securing his rights as inventor of the telephone, and on his twenty-ninth birthday the patent had arrived. One week later, March 10, 1876, the first distinct message was received over the wire.

At the Centennial Exposition, held in Philadelphia that year, the new invention was given its first public exhibition. People had come from all parts of the country and from distant lands to attend the Exposition and to view the wonderful developments made in the United States of America during the previous one hundred years. One day the Emperor of Brazil, Don Pedro, was persuaded to listen over the telephone. Upon putting the receiver to his ear he exclaimed excitedly, "It talks!"

Then his friend, Lord Kelvin, who was a leading electrical

scientist and the engineer of the Atlantic cable, also listened. "It does speak," he said.

One after another the distinguished men in that group took their turn at the strange, new instrument and were astonished to hear a human voice speaking over the wire. "This is the most remarkable thing I have seen in America," Lord Kelvin declared.

Although the telephone was highly praised by scientific men, other people were slow to realize its value. Even some businessmen thought it could never be made practical, and Bell was ridiculed as a "crank who says he can talk through a wire." It seemed absurd to think that one might speak into a tube or boxlike instrument and be heard at a distance through a similar looking instrument at the other end of a wire. Several close friends of the young inventor encouraged him to keep on trying, for they believed he had made a great discovery which would someday be appreciated. They furnished the money to continue his improvements and make the telephone of use to the world.

On the night of October 9, 1876, young Bell and his friend borrowed the use of the telegraph wire between Boston and Cambridge, attached their instruments at each end, and carried on the first long-distance conversation in the country, over a distance of two miles. Almost forty years later they used the same instruments and spoke over four thousand miles of wire, from San Francisco to New York. By that time the telephone had gained popularity until it was considered important to the interest of the public in all civilized lands.

When the world woke up to the value of this marvelous invention Alexander Graham Bell was not without honor. From Japan the Emperor bestowed on him the highest gift of recognition; from the Royal Society of Great Britain and the Society of Fine Arts of London he received medals. The government of France made him an officer of the Legion of Honor and awarded him the Volta prize of fifty thousand francs. This money he used when he founded the Volta Bureau in Washington "for the increase and diffusing of knowledge relating to the deaf." Never did he lose his interest in the deaf, although he devoted much of his time in later years to other research for the benefit of mankind. In a sense, the world owes to the deaf the invention of the telephone. If Bell had not studied every phase of sound in his preparation to teach deaf-mutes how to speak, he would not have been prepared to carry through the experiments that brought the telephone.

After a long, useful life Alexander Graham Bell died on Wednesday morning, August 2, 1922, at his summer home near Baddeck, Cape Breton, Nova Scotia. He was buried on the summit of Beinn Bhreagh in a grave blasted out of solid rock. During the simple ceremony on the mountaintop the entire telephone system of the United States and Canada, for the space of one minute, suspended service. There was silence over the wires in tribute to the man who had made telephone communication possible.

Chapter 4

ROSA BONHEUR

She Wanted Only to Paint

DID you ever try to eat when every swallow nearly choked you? Then you understand how shy, little Rosa Bonheur must have felt every time she sat down to eat her meals in the Fauborg St. Antoine School. There she was surrounded by girls who wore gay clothing and ate from silver mugs. Rosa's dress was calico, her shoes were coarse, and her mug was a tin cup. Moreover, she ate with an iron spoon!

Rosa resented the fact that she was the daughter of a poor man. Even more she resented the fact that she was being forced to attend school. What did she care about a gloomy dormitory, stuffy classrooms, and dry books when the great out-of-doors was calling. She felt like a prisoner shut up in a dungeon. She grew so listless that she came no longer to eat her meals, and soon afterwards she fell ill.

"Whatever shall I do with poor little Rosa?" pondered her father sadly, as he brought her home to get well. This was not the first time Rosa had failed him as a student. When her mother had died a few years earlier, he had sent Rosa and her two brothers to live with a kind woman who cared for them and sent them to school. But Rosa did not always follow the path that led into the schoolroom. When the sun shone bright and the out-of-doors seemed to be calling to her, sometimes she strayed away into the woods to play. She would return with her arms full of daisies and marigolds and her heart full of joy.

She did not mean to be a truant. She had gone to study in nature's schoolroom the kind of lessons she loved best. There she found plants, flowers, insects, and colors, colors, colors! Like a real artist she appreciated these lessons and studied them. But the kind woman who cared for her did not understand. She felt unhappy because little Rosa refused to attend school regularly.

This went on for some time. Then Rosa's father, Monsieur Bonheur, decided that if she refused to study in the schoolroom she must learn needlecraft. Rosa had never shown the slightest interest in such work, but her father supposed that such instruction was necessary in the proper education of his motherless child. He placed her in a sewing establishment, hoping that she might become a seamstress. How Rosa hated seams! She could see nothing beautiful in the stitches which her instructors tried to teach. All the while Rosa bent over her lessons she disliked them as much as the needle which constantly pricked her fingers! Only a short time did she remain in that school until she became sick and had to be sent home again.

All this happened before Rosa had been sent to the Fauborg St. Antoine School. And now for the third time she had failed her father as a student. Perplexed and disappointed, he decided to allow her to choose her own lessons. He was greatly surprised to find that she chose to copy whatever she saw him do in his art studio. Sometimes she made drawings. Sometimes she busied herself with modelings, her clever fingers fashioning each bit of work with remarkable skill. Now, she sang as she worked from morning until night. The merry sparkle danced again in her eyes. She was at last as happy as she could be.

"If my daughter chooses to become an artist," thought Monsieur Bonheur as he watched her at work, "I will teach her everything I know about art." With this resolution he began in earnest to show her how to do her work correctly. For years he had been giving drawing lessons in schools where he was poorly paid. Although a talented painter, he had no time to devote to his beloved work, for he had to teach in order to earn enough money to supply the necessities of his family. Now he cheerfully gave his spare time to teach Rosa how to make correct drawings.

Rosa never tired of her father's suggestions and instructions. She learned how to do her work so accurately that her father sent her to a famous studio near by to copy the works of old masters. With a happy heart she set out on this undertaking, and day after day she labored at her easel with her paints and brushes. So interested was she that she paid no attention to anything that was going on around her. This was the great work which she had longed to do all through her childhood, and to her it seemed as play. She was often tired after spending a long day in the famous studio, but she was never unhappy. Now she did not care that her dress was only a plain frock and that her shoes were coarse. She did not mind having to eat her meals from a tin cup with an iron spoon. The director of the Louvre, where she spent those busy days, said of her that he had never seen such steady effort and such great interest shown in one's work.

One day Rosa glanced up from her easel and saw an elderly gentleman standing near, looking intently at her copy. When he saw that she had raised her head, he spoke to her. "My child," said he, "your copy is superb, faultless. Work patiently as you have begun, and I prophesy that you will become a great artist." Then he passed on, but Rosa did not forget his words. "If that old man is correct in his prophesying," mused Rosa happily as she hurried home that evening, "I shall someday be an artist whom people will remember."

When Rosa finished her copies of the old masters she placed the paintings on the market, and one by one she sold them. Although she received only a small sum for this work, she was glad to be able to earn a little money to help her father. She then felt encouraged to keep on trying. Landscapes or historical paintings, she could reproduce upon the canvas with equal skill. But one day when she happened to paint a goat she was so pleased with the result that she decided to become a specialist in painting animals.

Rosa was now seventeen, and her father was still a poor man. He could not afford to furnish live models for her to use in this work; therefore, she decided to overcome this handicap by going out into the country where live models could be found on the farms, grazing in the pastures, or laboring in the fields. Shouldering her easel and other necessary equipment, and tucking a piece of bread into her pocket for lunch, she tramped for miles over the countryside in search of the objects which she wished to paint. Back and forth morning and evening she went. She was often dust-covered and weary, and she occasionally returned home at night drenched with rain and overburdened with mud clinging to her heavy shoes. In spite of these difficulties she kept painting, for she knew that success in any work cannot be won without earnest effort.

There were other unpleasant features about Rosa's work which she needed to struggle through in order to understand her task thoroughly. The time might come when she would need to paint an animal death scene on the canvas. Dearly as she loved animals, and much as she shrank from the sight of suffering, she felt that she must be prepared to depict such a scene with her paint and brushes. She went to the slaughter pens, set up her easel, and calmly and courageously worked while the butchers killed cattle and sheep for the market. Because of her quiet dignity and careful attention to her work, she was highly respected by the men who worked there. Sometimes they would come near and watch her, wondering at her skill and determination.

For a while Rosa's home was on the top floor of a six-story tenement house, and the family had the privilege of using the roof. There was no elevator to carry things up, but Rosa planted a small roof garden, where she had honeysuckles, sweet peas, nasturtiums, and a few vegetables. One day they brought a pet sheep to the middle of this gay little garden in the sky. Climbing up and down six flights of stairs is tiresome work in itself, but Rosa's younger brother often took the pet sheep on his back and carried it down to the ground where it could graze on the tender grass. Then he would carry it back again to its roof-garden home.

At the age of nineteen Rosa sent two pictures to the Fine Arts Exhibition, where they would be judged by the critics. Both pictures were good and attracted the attention of the public. The next year she sent three pictures, which were even better received than the others had been. And a few years later she exhibited twelve pictures at the same exhibition—some of her father's and brother's, as well as her own. By this time the critics were praising her work, for they recognized that she had the talent of a great artist.

The praise of critics inspired Rosa to work harder than ever. Several years later she presented a beautiful picture called "Cantal Oxen," for which she received the gold medal. This picture was purchased by England, and Rosa was honored as a great artist.

Her father, too, shared in her honors, for he had been her instructor. At once he was made director of a government school of design for girls. No longer did he need to struggle with poverty, for the promise of plenty came with his daughter's well-earned fame. His sons and daughters, now grown to maturity, all shared in his love of art. He realized at last that his years of toil and sacrifice had not been spent in vain. In the joy of his daughter's popularity he seemed to grow young again.

Rosa did not cease working hard when she had won for herself a place of honor among the artists of France. Although she had hoped to become famous, she had sought rather than fame the satisfaction which comes from giving to the world one's very best effort. Always she thought when viewing her latest painting, "I may be able to do better than this." Now orders for paintings came pouring in, and she continued to work as diligently as when she had been unknown and poor. For eighteen months she studied to paint a beautiful picture called "Horse Fair," and when at last the picture was finished and placed on exhibition, the critics called it her masterpiece. A wealthy English gentleman, seeing the picture, considered it valuable enough to pay eight thousand dollars for it, an unusually high sum at that time.

After the appearance and sale of this work of art, picture lovers on both sides of the Atlantic marveled at the rare skill of this young French artist. "She rightly deserves to be decorated with the Cross of the Legion of Honor," said some of her enthusiastic admirers. This badge of distinction which France confers upon her most worthy citizens had never been given to a woman, and Napoleon, fearing lest he would be criticized for thus honoring a woman, hesitated to present it to Rosa Bonheur. During his absence from Paris, the empress, acting as regent in his place, visited the studio of the famous girl artist one day and pinned the badge on her blouse.

Rosa continued to dress simply and to work hard after she became famous and wealthy. She appreciated the comforts of a good home, but she did not care for a life of ease. She gave away much of her income and was always ready to help raise funds to assist struggling artists. Of herself she said, "I have been a faithful student since I was ten years old. I have studied Nature, and expressed to the best of my ability the ideas and feelings with which she has inspired me. I felt within me the power to paint; I cultivated it, and have produced works that have won the favor of the great judges."

Rosa lived through the exciting days of the great war when Prussia conquered France, and her beautiful chateau lay in the path of the conquering army. But so great was the world's respect for her that the enemy did not molest any of her possessions. Rich and poor alike honored the great woman who went quietly about her beloved tasks and never felt herself superior to the humblest peasant. When Rosa Bonheur died at seventy-seven, she left the world a wealth of beautiful paintings to keep her memory alive.

Chapter 5

ELIZABETH BARRETT BROWNING

"The Priestess of Poetry"

FIVE miles south of Durham, England, in a country estate
called Coxhoe Hall, a wealthy West Indian merchant and
his young wife were living when their first child was born. The
child was welcomed joyfully by her parents, Mr. and Mrs. Edward Barrett, and every day they loved her more and more. Elizabeth was the name they chose to give her.

Elizabeth was still too young to remember her surroundings
when her father purchased a new home in Herefordshire, among
the Malvern Hills. Here at Hope End, the quiet country home,
Elizabeth grew to young womanhood. Here she welcomed the
arrival of sisters and brothers until there were ten of them—two
sisters and eight brothers. When Edward, the eldest brother,
began to talk he called Elizabeth "Ba." Thereafter the other

members of the family affectionately applied that name to her, and Elizabeth grew to love it as her pet name.

As a child, Elizabeth sometimes ran and played with her sisters and brothers in the grassy meadows, or climbed the beautiful hills, or roamed through the shady woodlands. The out-of-doors held a charm for her, and when she grew older and sorrows came into her life she felt comforted when she could take a walk in the fields. One day after taking such a walk she wrote a beautiful little poem, called "Out in the Fields with God":

> The little cares that fretted me,
>   I lost them yesterday,
> Among the fields, above the sea,
>   Among the winds at play;
> Among the lowing of the herds,
>   The rustling of the trees;
> Among the singing of the birds,
>   The humming of the bees.
>
> The foolish fears of what may happen,
>   I cast them all away
> Among the clover-scented grass,
>   Among the new-mown hay;
> Among the rustling of the corn,
>   Where drowsy poppies nod,
> Where ill thoughts die, and good are born—
>   Out in the fields with God.

Elizabeth was quite young when she began writing verses. As a little schoolgirl she was very fond of reading, and she spent many hours with her books when she should have been romping in the sunshine to build up a stronger body. Her love of reading grew greater as she grew older; and since she had access to only the best books, she formed a taste for reading good literature.

Instead of sending his children to school, Mr. Barrett engaged teachers to instruct them at home. He was careful to provide only the best teachers, and Elizabeth received a liberal education. When her favorite brother, Edward, was urged to study Greek she volunteered to share his studies with him. She had been wishing to be able to read the stories of those ancient Greeks, in the original language. And she knew that the New Testament, too, was first written in Greek before it was translated into Latin and German and English. She wanted to be able to read it as it had been written so long ago. With these desires to urge her on she struggled through her lessons in Greek until she became a good scholar and was able to read the language with ease.

Not far from Elizabeth's childhood home was the town of Great Malvern, where many friends of the Barrett family lived. Among them were the Boyds, who were Christian people, well educated and fond of reading. When they heard that Elizabeth was studying Greek, Mr. Boyd began to take a special interest in her. Although he was blind he understood the Greek language as well as a professor. He invited Elizabeth to his home often and asked her to read to him. Together they would pore over old Greek manuscripts.

Through the influence of Mr. Boyd, Elizabeth became acquainted with the history of the old church fathers, and she read about them with much interest. She enjoyed the mythical stories of the Greek classics, too, for they appealed to her youthful imagination. She used to sit alone under the shade trees near her home and read Greek stories until her head would ache. Sometimes she would dream about the ancient heroes of Greece and weave little rhymes about them. When she was thirteen years old, she wrote a long poem called "The Battle of Marathon." Her father was very proud of this literary work and had fifty copies printed. He believed that his little daughter was a literary genius.

One of Elizabeth's favorite recreations was horseback riding. In her father's stables were riding horses which the children might use whenever they chose to go out. One day Elizabeth hurried out for a ride and tried to saddle up alone. This task was unfamiliar to her, and she failed to fasten and tighten the girth properly. When she mounted the saddle, it slipped. She fell to the ground, bringing the saddle on top of her. A long time passed before she was able to go riding again, for she was severely injured by the fall. While she was in bed she found much comfort in her books. And when she grew tired of reading she sometimes wrote verses for her own amusement.

There came a sad day in the home at Hope End when members of the household spoke in subdued voices and tiptoed from room to room, for the beloved invalid mother lay dying. After she was gone it seemed for a time that the joy of life had gone out, too. The home at Hope End was never the same again, and a few years later Mr. Barrett moved his family to the south of England, where they located at Sidmouth, on the seashore.

Although it was hard for Elizabeth to leave all her dear friends, she soon learned to love her new home and surroundings. She never grew tired of looking out of the windows and watching the waves dance in the sunlight and dash against the shore. The sea breeze seemed to strengthen her frail body and to enliven her spirits. Remembering her former friends, she wrote long letters to them, telling about her new home and interests in Sidmouth. She also told them about herself and the work in which she was beginning to take a lively interest. Now she began to write long poems for publication. The Barrett family lived in Sidmouth for three years; then they moved to London.

The change from the beautiful landscapes and broad sea views to the crowded streets of a great city seemed to smother the spirits of the Barrett children when they first came to live in London. Elizabeth suffered most, for she missed the pure breezes from the sea as well as the beautiful scenery. Not long after they came to the city she became ill, and ever afterwards she remained an invalid. She spent several years in her room where only a few close friends were admitted to see her. During those years, however, she continued to make new friends. Those were the pen-and-ink friends who, reading her splendid poems in the best literary magazines of the day, wrote to tell her of their appreciation. When she answered their letters, they wrote again and again. In this way their friendships grew.

In London, Elizabeth was overjoyed to find her old friend, the blind Mr. Boyd. He, too, had come to the great city to make his home. Because of Elizabeth's ill health these two friends seldom met, but they took the deepest interest in each other. In her room Elizabeth would pen cheery letters to Mr. Boyd, telling about the things which would interest him. Sometimes she would send her latest poems for him to read; sometimes she would exchange books and magazines with him. Her sister often carried these letters to Mr. Boyd, but occasionally a servant delivered them. Then he always sent a reply back to her in the same manner, and thus they helped to brighten each other's dreary lives.

The time came when Elizabeth's physician advised that she be moved to a warmer climate for the winter periods. Her father then sent her to Torquay, on the extreme southern coast of England, to spend the winter. Edward, her favorite brother and companion during childhood, went with her to keep her company. Occasionally other members of the family came down to visit them. Thus passed the first winter by the sea. Springtime came, but since Elizabeth was too frail to undertake the journey back to London, she and her brother remained in Torquay. She was placed under the care of the best physicians; still her health remained in a critical state. Sometimes she longed to return to London, even with its fog and narrow streets, for she wished to be with her family and friends again.

During her second summer in Torquay another great sorrow came into Elizabeth's life. One warm day her brother and two friends went out in a small boat to row across the bay, and when they were some distance from the shore the boat floundered and upset, drowning the three men. Never again could Elizabeth enjoy the murmur of the sea, and now she wanted to leave Torquay at once. The longing to return home was almost too much, but Elizabeth was too ill to travel and had to spend another year at the seaside. Then her father sent a specially built carriage with a bed in it, and she was taken back to London.

Although an invalid, and often unable to leave her bed for long at a time, Elizabeth continued her work of writing. Her poems were received with pleasure by the editors of the best literary papers, and her name appeared among the most noted authors of the time. Some of these famous people she had the pleasure of meeting. There was Wordsworth, the poet laureate of England, whose writings she admired very much. She came to know Alfred Tennyson, a young poet who succeeded Wordsworth in the place of national honor when that aged poet died. And there was Robert Browning, whom, after a friendship of several years, she married.

Elizabeth seldom had the opportunity of going about in London because of her ill health, but she heard much about the conditions of life among the people in that city and all through her native country. She knew about some of the evils which were spoiling the lives of many of her fellow men. Although she was protected from the sorrows of poverty, she felt pity for the poor and unfortunate. She believed that the lawmakers of England could remedy some of the evils if they would try. Very bravely she set to work and wrote a poem called "The Cry of the Children." In it she pictured the wrong of forced child labor, which her country then allowed. The following lines are from that poem:

> Do you hear the children weeping, O my brothers,
>   Ere the sorrow comes with years?
> They are leaning their young heads against their mothers,
>   And that cannot stop their tears.
> The young lambs are bleating in the meadows;
>   The young birds are chirping in the nest;
> The young fawns are playing with the shadows;
>   The young flowers are blowing towards the west—
> But the young, young children, O my brothers!
>   They are weeping bitterly!
> They are weeping in the playtime of the others,
>   In the country of the free.

Although Elizabeth had been an invalid for years and years, seldom able to leave her room, one day she was asked by another famous poet, Robert Browning, to become his wife. Not for a long time would she consent to marry him, but finally she did, and they were married in London. Very soon afterwards they went away to Europe, to make their home beneath the sunny skies of Italy. Here they lived happily for fifteen years. They continued the work they loved to do and met other famous artists who went to stay awhile in Italy. Sometimes they returned to visit in England, but they preferred to make their home in the warmer climate of southern Europe. There Elizabeth did not suffer from damp and cold weather. Sometimes she was strong enough to go with her husband on hikes into the woods and on horseback up steep mountain passes.

Famous persons, we are told, express their highest selves in their literary work. Friends of Elizabeth Barrett Browning said of her that in everyday life she was the same beautiful character whose excellence shone through the work of her pen. Always she was strong in the defense of truth and right, earnest in her endeavors, and indignant against all kinds of wrong.

While she loved the beautiful, she did not close her eyes to scenes of misery where she could help ease suffering. Among her best poems we find "Sonnets from the Portuguese," "Cowper's Grave," "Dead Pan," and "Aurora Leigh."

In spite of her long struggle with frail health, Elizabeth Barrett Browning lived to be fifty-five years old. In 1861 she died at her home in Italy.

Chapter 6

LUTHER BURBANK

His Fame Grew in a Garden

IN A large, brick farmhouse, set some distance back from the
road that led to the village of Lancaster, Massachusetts,
lived the happy Burbank family. Already there were twelve
boys and girls in that household when, on March 7, 1849, a
baby brother was born.

Near the farmhouse was a flower garden which was the
special pride of Mrs. Burbank. When baby Luther grew old
enough to toddle about she used to take him with her into the
garden to admire the pretty blossoms. Never did he tear their
brightly colored petals apart as babies usually do. Instead, if a
petal fell he would try hard to replace it. He enjoyed watching
the bees, butterflies, and hummingbirds flit about from flower
to flower, gathering food and making themselves at home among
the blossoms.

One of Luther's odd playthings when he was a wee child was a lobster cactus in a pot. This he used to carry about and play with as other boys would play with a ball. One day while carrying it he stumbled and fell. He broke the pot and the plant and almost his heart as well. Whether or not he recalled this incident when he grew to be a man we do not know. But long afterwards, when he had become a naturalist, he spent ten years developing from the wild desert cactus a plant without spines or "prickles," which makes excellent food for cattle.

Luther loved not only the well-cultivated flowers which bloomed in his mother's garden, but the wild buttercups, goldenrods, and plain little field daisies, too. He disliked hearing the daisies called a pest, and resolved that some day he would teach them how to become beautiful, respectable flowers that people would welcome in their gardens. Sure enough, one of his achievements was the cultivation of the common field daisy into a garden flower, the Shasta daisy.

Early in the springtime Luther used to be on hand when the dry, lifeless-looking bulbs were brought out from the cellar and placed in the earth. He would watch for the first tiny green shoots as they sprang up, and continued his observations until the flower stalks bloomed into iris, daffodils, and tulips.

Flowers were not the only plants that claimed Luther's attention and interest. The vegetable garden also fascinated him while as a farm boy he pulled weeds and hoed corn and watched the plant life grow and change. When seed-gathering time came he noticed that always seeds were selected from the first large, ripe tomato, the finest melon, the most perfect ear of corn—always from the best of everything. This principle of selection was the first rule of plant improvement Luther observed. The seed-planting season was another event. He learned that some seeds are sown directly in the earth while others must first be cared for in hotbeds or boxes made for that purpose and later transplanted in the soil when the warm sunshine has taken the frost out of the ground.

Boylike, Luther sometimes mixed play with his work. When the early lettuce peeped out of the ground in green letters spelling L-u-t-h-e-r, one did not need to guess who had sown the lettuce seed. When a large cucumber was found hidden among the leaves in a glass bottle having such a narrow neck that it barely admitted the slender vine, no one was at a loss to know who had placed the tiny cucumber in the glass prison to watch its development day after day. And when the initials *L. B.* were found traced on little pumpkins, Luther was merely wanting to see those letters increase in size as the pumpkins grew larger. Once, after having watched a circus parade pass by, Luther traced on the little pumpkins outlines of elephants, lions, tigers, and other circus symbols; and when those same pumpkins grew up they were taken to the county fair and put on display.

At school Luther was shy and timid. But as he grew older he became the leader in the little band of barefoot boys who searched throughout the meadow and woodland pasture for nature's treasured store of nuts and wild fruits. He knew where the sweetest strawberries hid in the meadow grasses, where the biggest blueberries grew in the pasture, and just where to find the best chestnuts and hickory nuts.

Luther used to examine the tiny mosses and lichens that grew on old stone walls, and wish that he might study them with the aid of a magnifying glass. When he grew old enough to earn money for himself, one of the first things he purchased was a microscope. Then he found great delight in studying nature and discovering beauty in flowers and mosses that is hidden from the unaided eye. He liked to read books of science and compare the facts read in books with the facts which he learned in the out-of-doors.

At the age of fifteen Luther enrolled as a student at the Lancaster Academy, where he continued his studies for several winters. He walked to school each day a distance of three miles, and often retraced his steps in the evening to enjoy an hour's practice in the gymnasium. During the summer months he worked in Worcester learning the mechanic's trade. Here he became a skilled worker. Still, he would have preferred to be working outside, soiling his hands with earth rather than the grease of a mechanic's shop. He paid close attention to the machinery in the shop, and one day he thought of an improvement which would mean a great deal to his employer. He carefully worked out a model and presented it to his employer, who was pleased with Luther's suggestion and offered to increase his salary. How surprised the man must have been when Luther quietly said, "No thank you. I'm going back to the farm to do the kind of work I like best."

A person does not become a great naturalist all at once. Much study, patience, and practice is required to try out experiments. But Luther Burbank's first great experiment in plant growing made him famous even though he was still a young man. He had read an article in the county newspaper concerning the inferior quality of the potatoes then raised. The thought occurred to him to begin his experiments with the potato.

When he found a seed ball on one of his potato plants he decided to watch carefully until the seeds would be ready to leave the mother plant. From that seed ball he took twenty-six tiny seeds so small that ten of them were not as large as an ordinary pinhead. These he saved until the following spring; then he planted them and waited through the long summer for the vines to grow and the potatoes to form. Only three of the seeds failed to grow; the others grew and behaved as potato plants should, and when time for digging came Luther found a few potatoes in each hill.

Luther took the potatoes from one hill to the agricultural fair held in the neighborhood. There he met one of the greatest seedmen of the United States, who became attracted to his experiment. "Continue testing this potato," the man said, "and if they prove to be as good as they look, I will buy them."

After three years of further testing Luther sent the potatoes to the seedman and received one hundred and fifty dollars for his new development. The new potato was called "Burbank" in honor of its originator. The Burbank potato withstood the blight and other diseases which attack vegetable plants much better than other varieties of potatoes. Ireland, the great potato-growing country, was pleased to receive some of the new Burbank potatoes. Soon the Irish peasants were growing potatoes of much better quality, and this greatly helped that country's food supply.

Not long after his first successful experiment, Luther Burbank decided to leave his home in Massachusetts and go to a warmer climate to continue his work. He crossed the continent to Santa Rosa, California. Here he became ill and unable to continue his work. Recovering from his illness took all the money he had saved. When he finally felt his health returning he was glad to move into an empty chicken house and work at whatever odd job he could get. He continued to be hopeful, and slowly he regained his health. Finally he was able to earn enough money to buy some land and begin again the work that he loved best.

Many years have passed since Luther Burbank created a rare garden spot in his southern California home. During these years wonderful things have taken place in that garden. Strange plants have come from the gardens of Italy, Japan, Siberia, India,

Australia, Patagonia, Alaska, New Zealand, China, and South America. These plants were brought to be changed and improved so that they might be of greater worth to the world.

Under the watchful eye and patient skill of Luther Burbank, some of the flowers were induced to change the color of their dresses, some to drop their bad habits, others to develop sweet perfumes. Some sour fruits were trained to become sweet. Good-for-nothing berries were made edible. And bitter nuts were developed into something good to eat. Millions of plants—grasses, flowers, vegetables, grains, and trees—passed through Burbank's hands. From these he selected a few to develop to such a point that they became pleasing food or beautiful ornaments or otherwise useful for the service of mankind.

No wonder people called this man, who accomplished so many wonders in the vegetable kingdom, the "Plant Wizard." To those who knew him best Luther Burbank was always a sincere, modest, ever-busy man with a great mission to fulfill on earth. Succeeding generations of the human race will continue in debt to this faithful worker whose skill has beautified gardens, improved the flavor and selling qualities of fruits, and made vegetables more flavorful and abundant. Of him it has been written:

> He walked with Patience many a tedious hour,
> With Genius' glowing lamp aflame in hand;
> Or sat with her in Wisdom's citadel,
> And heard the watchman calling, "All is well";
> Then saw the shrunken, blighted bloom expand
> Into a graceful, snowy, starry flower.

Chapter 7

WILLIAM CAREY

Preacher, Teacher, and Translator

IN A hollow at the end of the village of Paulers Pury, Northamptonshire, England, stood a plain cottage where lived a poor weaver and his young wife. One summer day in 1761 a son, whom they named William, was born.

For six years little William Carey's smiles and childish prattle brought sunshine into the plain little cottage in the hollow while his father sat at the hand loom weaving cloth or worked in the garden near by. Then one day the mover's wagon came and carried everything away from the place to unload it before the door of the schoolhouse that stood on the hill up in the village. Little William understood that his father, Edmund Carey, was to become the schoolmaster of the village and that he would be permitted to attend school. At that time there was no free public school for the children of the village. Because William's father was one of the educated men of the village, knowing how to read, write, and cipher, he was chosen to take the place of the teacher who had moved from the village to another town.

The schoolhouse was just a large house in which the master and his family lived. One room of the building was reserved for the schoolroom. Here the children who met to study had no desks; the only furnishings of the room were benches made of rough tree slabs. In spite of this poor equipment, little William and his school companions learned how to read, write, and do mathematical sums. Here they also memorized the catechism, which was a part of their religious teaching.

William was a student of the out-of-doors as well as of books. He loved plant life and the wild insects and birds that live in the open spaces. He enjoyed going on hikes through the woodlands which bordered the village, and down the dusty lanes or across the meadows in search of wild flowers, insects, and birds. His mother, understanding his love of nature, permitted him to stock his bedroom with his collections. By closely watching them he learned the habits of the birds, insects, and plants which he studied. While still a boy he was recognized as the best-informed person in the village on natural history, for when anyone discovered an unusual bird, insect, or flower unknown to the other villagers, they would say, "Take it to Bill Carey; he can tell you about it."

Because he was short William often had to climb trees in order to observe the habits of his out-of-door friends. One day when climbing a difficult tree he fell and injured himself. For several days he suffered from the injuries and had to stay in bed, but almost the first thing he did as soon as he was able to get about again was to tackle that same tree and climb it successfully. He was a boy who believed "I can." If he failed the first time, he kept on trying until he did what he set out to do.

William did not spend all his time in the schoolroom or at play. He carried water from the spring down the lane at the foot of the hill, and he brought firewood from the forest outside the village. These tasks led him along nature's trails, where he used to keep his eyes open to learn her secrets. Sometimes he would take his little sister along to show her a rare plant that he had found, or to gather wild flowers.

William was quite young when his uncle, Peter Carey, returned to the village after an absence of many years. He was quite a hero. He had been a soldier in the new world, America, and he told many thrilling tales about Canada's Indians, about the war with the French and the capture of Quebec, and adventures on the seas. Listening to these tales, William felt a longing to learn more about lands across the seas and of strange peoples. This interest in people of other lands had been shown before this time through his memorizing pages and pages of foreign words, and his interest in other languages.

Books were not so numerous when William was a boy. The few he read were of scientific interest or of human interest adventures in travel. He talked so much of Columbus, the discoverer of America, that his companions nicknamed him after his hero. The adventures of Robinson Crusoe thrilled him as much as such tales excite boys and girls of today.

The schoolroom door swung shut behind William for the last time when he was only twelve, for he had finished the grades in the villages school and his parents were too poor to send him away to continue his studies elsewhere. The time had come when he must begin to work for a livelihood and prepare to be a man. But this did not mean that William stopped studying. Whenever he had a spare moment and a good book to read he added to his knowledge.

When William left the schoolroom of his boyhood he planned

to become a gardner, like his hero-uncle, Peter. He loved plant life and was eager to cultivate the fields and raise food products. For two years he followed the plow along the furrows and watched the growth of his garden. During those years he suffered so much from sunburn that he could hardly sleep at night, and his father decided to train him for other work. So William was sent to work for a shoemaker who lived in a neighboring village.

William was expected to work for seven years in this shoemaker's employ. Boys placed in shops like that to learn trades were called apprentices. An older boy, named John Warr, also worked for William's employer, and the two boys spent much time together. John was kind and thoughtful and took time to help William learn shoecraft. He also talked to his young friend about God and the Christian way of living. Learning about the Christian way and accepting that way for himself proved to be the happiest discovery of William's lifetime.

In his spare moments William used to examine the books on his master's shelf. One day he found in a New Testament commentary some strange letters which he supposed must certainly represent another language. No one about the shop could explain their meaning to him. Determined to find out, William copied them with great care and took them home on his next visit to Paulers Pury. There he found a man whom he knew had once been a student of ancient languages. He showed the letters to him. "Do you know what language these letters represent?"

"Yes," replied the man, "that is Greek." Then the man gave William his first lessons in Greek. William also studied Latin, Hebrew, Italian, and Dutch, and learned how to use these languages. All of this he did while working as a shoe cobbler.

When William grew to manhood he continued to work as a shoe cobbler, but he also began to preach to the people in the village where he lived. Sometimes he visited other villages and preached in them also. During these years he began to think a great deal about the people who lived in countries where the true God was not known. He believed that they, too, should be taught about God. He began to study the geographical location of other countries, and drew a large map of the world which he hung on the walls of his workshop. Every day as he cobbled shoes that map hung before him, reminding him of the millions of people who knew nothing about the God whom he loved and served.

Not only did William think a great deal about the people in other lands; he also talked about them. Other ministers at that time believed the "notion" of trying to convert the heathen was foolish. At last some of them began to understand that William was right. "God expects us to take the gospel to the people of every nation," William said again and again. "I will go as a missionary if the church will help me." For several years he waited, hoping to go to the islands in the South Pacific. During those years he kept busy working as a shoe cobbler to support his family, studying languages, and preaching on Sundays.

At last a call came for someone to go to India to begin missionary work there. William Carey was ready to answer that call. Taking his wife and four children, he sailed away from England on June 13, 1793.

After five months of sailing they at last reached India. There William Carey found that his first task would be to learn the language of the people. He set to work to study the principal language of that part of India where they were stationed. This language is called the Bengali. He soon found that different languages are spoken in different parts of the country and that he would need to know several languages if he wished to travel about and preach. As soon as he learned the Bengali well enough to understand its meaning he began to write the Bible, word for word, in that language. What a task this was!

When William was ready to print the first Bible in the language of India he found that he did not have enough money to do the work. More time was spent waiting and hoping that help would come. Then a friend who knew of his desire gave him a printing press. How excited he and his helpers were to set it up and learn how to use it! They worked so earnestly at the press that some of their Bengali neighbors, looking on, thought the press was their idol. Little did those idol worshipers realize that the hand press was going to help break down idol worship in India.

After living in India only seven years William could speak the Bengali language so fluently that he was asked to teach in the first college founded in that country. He and his Indian helpers had to write a Bengali grammar and other textbooks to use in the college. During this time he kept on studying other Indian languages also, and soon he was teaching three of them to the college students.

Not only did William Carey study languages and teach in the college at Calcutta and preach whenever he could, he also found time to work in a garden near his home. Here he spent many happy hours among his flowers and plants. He also watched the birds and insects of that country and studied their habits. This out-of-door occupation benefited his health and made him stronger for his indoor work. Many visitors from other lands were delighted to walk through the garden of this first missionary to India, whose love of nature continued as long as he lived.

Although William Carey taught in the college for many years, he kept his mind on the great need which had brought him from his homeland. Year after year he worked at the great task which he had first set out to do. That task was giving to the people of India the Bible in their own tongue. There were so many languages to master that any other person might have become discouraged; but William never gave up. After years of hard work he had printed the whole Bible in six different languages. Still he kept on, and by and by he had translated the New Testament and part of the Old Testament into five more languages, the entire New Testament into eighteen other languages, and the Gospels into five others. This made thirty-four languages into which he had written the whole or parts of the Bible.

Besides giving the Bible to millions of India's people, William Carey also had the joy of giving three sons as missionaries to that land. They grew up to love the work their father was doing and the people they lived among. It was only natural that they should carry on this important work.

After spending forty-one years in India, William Carey died in that land. He had made the work far easier for other missionaries who would follow him to that country, for they would find the Bible already waiting in the languages of the people. They would find people who had been prepared to receive Christianity.

Chapter 8

FANNY CROSBY

Her Songs Will Always Be Sung

"AUNT FANNY," called a cheery voice, "here comes the postman with a letter for you!"

"Where is it from?" asked the dear old lady, never stopping her knitting to adjust her spectacles, for she knew she could not read it.

"It bears a foreign postmark—England, I believe."

"Then by all means read it at once," urged Aunt Fanny.

"Oh, it's a poem," exclaimed her friend, as soon as she had torn open the envelope and unfolded its contents, "from that wonderful woman in England, Frances Ridley Havergal."

The poem began:

> Sweet blind singer over the sea,
> Tuneful and jubilant; how can it be,
> That the songs of gladness, which float so far,

As if they fell from the evening star,
Are the notes of one who never may see?

And while it was being read the old lady sat very still in her low rocking chair, smiling happily. She felt pleased to hear how much her songs were being appreciated and sung in England.

Fanny Jane Crosby, the hymn writer, was blind. She had been blind ever since she was a tiny baby, only a few weeks old. In spite of this affliction she had grown up to become a cheerful, lovable, and noble Christian, and she wrote some of the most beautiful hymns that the world has ever sung. How did she do it? Perhaps we can answer that question when we recall the story of her life.

The rural cottage in which Fanny Jane Crosby was born on March 24, 1820, stood near the bank of a gay little brook that rambled through Putnam County, New York. Fanny's parents were poor, although they and their ancestors were numbered among the brave New England families who helped to make America great. Fanny could not remember her father, for he died before she was a year old. Then her grandmother, a dear Christian woman, came to live in the little cottage and care for the blind baby while her mother was at work.

As baby Fan grew older she often sat on her grandmother's knee, listening to stories about the wonderful world in which she lived. Grandmother knew Fan could never see the beauties of nature with her eyes, and she wanted the child to begin early to see them with her imagination. She wanted to train little Fan to think about the word pictures which she tried to paint so patiently, day after day.

And so it was through Grandmother's stories that Fanny caught her first idea of the sunrise and sunset pictures. She learned about the twinkling stars, and about the silvery moon which rides around the earth. She learned about the clouds with their various shapes and colors—the fleecy white summer clouds, the murky rain clouds, and the dark storm clouds. She learned about the beautiful rainbow, too, which God placed in the sky as a bow of promise to mankind.

From Grandmother, Fanny also learned about the little feathered songsters that came every springtime to nest in the shade trees near by. Together they would listen to the birds sing, and then Grandmother would explain how each bird looked. Soon Fanny learned how to recognize each bird by its song. "Oh, there is a meadow lark!" she would shout, just as happy as if she could see him balancing himself on the slender twig. One day Fanny heard an unfamiliar bird call down in the meadow. "Grandmother," she cried excitedly, "come and listen! A new bird is here."

"He is saying, 'Whippoorwill'!" exclaimed Grandmother, "and that is how he got his name." Then she told little Fan that he had mottled wings and a reddish brown breast and a white, bristled tail. Thus one at a time Fanny came to know the mockingbird, the redheaded woodpecker, the robin, the red-winged blackbird, the song sparrow, the meadow lark, the goldfinch, the yellow warbler, and the wren.

In pleasant weather Grandmother often took Fanny for long walks. Sometimes they stopped to examine gay wild flowers on the hill, to pick violets down by the brook, or to gather bouquets of apple, cherry, and peach blossoms in the orchard. Fanny examined every kind of blossom carefully while Grandmother told its name and described its color.

When Fanny grew old enough to romp and play she learned how to find her way alone through the grassy meadow. She learned how to ride horseback, how to climb rail fences, and even how to walk the top rail! One day her mother brought home from the pasture a shivering little lamb. Fanny had been wishing for a pet, and so she begged to have the lamb for her very own. "I cannot give it to you to keep always," said her mother, "but you may care for it and play with it until it grows up." Then she told Fanny the rhyme story about "Mary's Little Lamb." This story pleased Fanny, and she too, soon trained her pet to follow her wherever she went. When the pet lamb grew up to be a sheep it had to be sold. Then a lonely little girl went to bed one night and cried herself to sleep!

Fanny never had much time to waste shedding tears. She soon found other things to occupy her time. Fanny began to make rhymes when she was a very little girl. She loved the musical rhythm of poetry. One day her mother told her that some of the world's greatest poets were blind. She read to Fanny the lines which Milton wrote on his blindness, and Fanny learned to repeat them from memory. When still very young she wrote these lines:

> Oh, what a happy soul am I!
> Although I cannot see,
> I am resolved that in this world
> Contented I will be.
>
> How many blessings I enjoy
> That other people don't;
> To weep and sigh because I'm blind
> I cannot, and I won't!

Because Fanny's mother was a very busy person, her grandmother continued to be her most constant teacher. From Grandmother she learned much about the love of the heavenly Father. With Grandmother's assistance she memorized many parts of the Bible. "Child, you will never be able to take the Book from the shelf and read it, as I do," Grandmother would say, "but you can store much of it in your bright mind, and then it will be with you wherever you go." With this encouragement Fanny studied until she could repeat from memory many of the Psalms, the Proverbs of Solomon, the Book of Ruth, and much of the New Testament. The stories of the Old Testament she knew word for word. All through her lifetime she prized these memory treasures which her dear old grandmother had helped her to store away. One day she wrote these lines about the Bible:

O Book, that with reverence I honor,
  What joy in thy pages I see!
O Book of my childhood devotion,
  More precious than rubies to me.

"How splendid it would be," thought Fanny one day, "if I could read for myself!" But there was no school for the blind near her home, and the expense of sending her away to school was more than her mother could afford. Fanny continued to learn from hearing others read and explain the meaning of things which she could not see. However, the desire to study in a school for the blind grew stronger in Fanny's heart every day, and she began to talk to the heavenly Father in prayer about this desire. She believed that he could help her mother find a way to send her to school. Then one morning her mother said, "Fanny, we shall begin preparations today to send you to the Institution for the Blind in New York city."

Schooldays brought new experiences to the sightless girl. She had never been alone among strangers before, and we may be sure that at first she felt homesick. The unfamiliar rooms and halls had to be explored little by little. Soon she became self-confident and knew her way around her new surroundings. She enjoyed the companionship of other young people who, like herself, were searching after knowledge with unseeing eyes. She studied her lessons eagerly and listened most attentively to the beautiful poetry which her teachers often read. As soon as she was able to choose her own reading she began a careful study of poetry.

At first Fanny's teachers did not encourage her to write rhymes. They thought she spent too much time with poetry, and occasionally they would assign her other work and take the poetry from her. This made her feel very unhappy. Then one day a doctor from Boston, who came to the Institution to examine the pupils, said to Fanny's teachers: "You will do well to teach this pupil to appreciate the finest there is in poetry. Read the best books to her, and give her every possible encouragement. You will hear from this young lady someday."

Fanny was delighted. Now she knew her teachers would no longer discourage her in doing what she liked best of all to do. They would help her when she tried to write rhymes. She felt that this was the happiest moment of her school life, and she began more earnestly than ever to study and write.

Everything seemed to be going along pleasantly with Fanny now. Her classmates were saying flattering things about her poems, and words of commendation were coming from other people, too. Fanny was feeling very pleased with herself when one day a teacher asked her to remain after class. She felt sure that he was going to say something good about her poems, as everyone else was doing. To her surprise, he began to talk to her about the harm which sometimes results from receiving too much flattery. He kindly showed her that her poems were weak in some places, and that they could not honestly be ranked with the best poetry. Fanny listened quietly, feeling very much ashamed. When he finished, she thanked him, dried her tears, and made up her mind to profit by his criticism.

For twelve years Fanny studied in the Institution, spending much time with music, art, and literature. Then she accepted a position as teacher in the same school, and remained eleven years longer. At once she became a favorite teacher, for she always encouraged her pupils to do their best. She was cheerful and patient, and understood their struggles because she had passed through similar struggles herself.

Fanny's love for sacred music had begun when she was a very small child. She used to think that the birds were singing songs of praise to their Creator and that the brook which flowed along sang His praises too. She felt that she would like to sing words of her own which she had put together into rhyme. The time came when she began to write such words; and the words were set to music. Then she heard them sung by others, too, wherever she attended religious services. She was made very happy when she heard that the world was singing her songs of praise and worship to God. Her hymns were translated into other languages and sung all around the world.

Fanny's first hymn to win world-wide favor was, "Pass Me Not, O Gentle Savior." Missionaries carried it across the seas and translated the words into the languages of the people among whom they labored. Thus Chinese and Japanese Christians began to sing the hymn just as enthusiastically as their brothers and sisters in America did.

One of Fanny Crosby's best-loved hymns came to be written this way: Mr. Doane, a gentleman who composed sacred music, said to her one day, "I have a tune that I should like to have you write words for."

He played the melody softly, and Fanny said, "That seems to be saying, 'Safe in the arms of Jesus.'" She hurried to her room, and there she wrote the beautiful words which we sing in this hymn.

Sometimes the blind hymnwriter visited missions in crowded cities and spoke to the people assembled there. One hot August evening she attended the services at the Bowery Mission in New

York city. Although unable to see the audience, she felt that she was addressing some young man who had been reared in a Christian home but had wandered far from its teachings. At the close of her address she said, "If there is a lad here tonight who has wandered away from his mother's teachings, I should like to meet him after the service." Sure enough, a boy about eighteen years old came forward and said, "Did you mean me?" He told her that he had promised his dying mother to live as she had taught him, but that he had not kept his promise. Fanny talked earnestly with him; then they knelt to pray. Later that same night, she wrote the words of this familiar song:

> Rescue the perishing, care for the dying,
> Snatch them in pity from sin and the grave;
> Weep o'er the erring one, lift up the fallen,
> Tell them of Jesus, the mighty to save.

This song is numbered among the five most famous of her writings which are sung in many lands. The others are: "Blessed Assurance, Jesus Is Mine!" "Pass Me Not, O Gentle Savior," "Safe in the Arms of Jesus," and "Saved by Grace."

One evening a traveler in the Sahara Desert heard a familiar melody floating to him from a distant campfire around which sat a group of rough-looking Bedouins. He had been dreading the prospect of spending a night in the desert among these fierce men, but when he heard their song he urged his camel along with all possible speed; for the men were singing one of Fanny Crosby's hymns! However rough-looking they were, he knew that they had come into contact with Christianity and that their hearts had been touched by the love of God.

Fanny Crosby lived to be ninety-four years old. In all, she wrote over eight thousand hymns. Some of them will be sung to the end of time.

Chapter 9

MARIE CURIE

Scientist and Patriot

T HE American children who proudly sing: "My country, 'tis of thee, sweet land . . . of thee I sing," are not the only children in the world who love the land of their birth better than any other land under the broad expanse of sky. Little Marie Sklodowska, the heroine of our story, was born in Warsaw, Poland, on November 7, 1867, and grew up with pride for her country in her heart. Although Poland fell prey to the greed of neighboring countries and was torn to pieces by them, the Polish people remained loyal in heart to their own nation and looked hopefully forward to the time when they would be reunited again under one flag.

Marie was still a small child when her mother died, leaving their home a sad place. There remained a sister, a brother, and an adorable father, but none of these could take the place of

Mother in the home. Marie cared less and less about staying at home. Every morning after finishing her breakfast she put on her cap and coat and hurried out the door to go as fast as her feet would carry her to her father's laboratory. Here she felt contented and happy, forgetting the great loss which had saddened her young heart. Marie enjoyed watching her father and asking questions about his work. She learned how to handle the test tubes and other delicate instruments with proper care, and soon her father allowed her to assist him. He called her his little helper and praised her for doing so well the little things he requested. Work with her father meant to Marie what play means to most children, and she enjoyed it from morning until evening.

Recognizing her unusual love for science, Marie's father encouraged her in that line of study. But he knew that she needed to be taught along other lines too if she hoped someday to become a scientist. When she grew old enough to enter the schoolroom he sent her there to study lessons from books, just as other children were doing.

Patriotic little Marie was displeased when the teacher said there could be no lessons in the Polish language. By order of the Russian government, into whose hands that part of Poland fell, the children were forced to study the Russian language in school. They were not allowed to speak in the Polish language to their teachers. Neither were they allowed to read the literature of their own nation nor to study its sad history. Police were stationed everywhere through the city to see that the orders of the Russian government were obeyed. It is no wonder that the Polish citizens of Warsaw were unhappy. As Marie grew older she understood better the distress of her countrymen, and she shared the bitter resentment which loyal Polish people felt toward the oppressing nation.

Many young Polish students in the Warsaw University felt that the Russian government was trying to crush out their love of Poland. Some of them decided to plan a revolution and make an attempt to regain their independence. They knew they were taking a great risk, for if their plans would be exposed they would be punished. They knew the Russian government had no patience with revolutionists and that even innocent persons had been suspected of disloyalty to their orders and had been cruelly punished. Still they dared to proceed with their plans.

When Marie grew old enough to take an interest in public affairs she joined the student revolutionists. She knew that a woman revolutionist would receive no more mercy from the Russian government than would a man, and that her sufferings might be greater if she should be found out.

One day the ever-watchful police heard about the students' plan. And Marie was told that they were likely to seize her with other suspects and banish her to faraway Siberia. Not wishing to fall into the hands of the Russian government, Marie decided to leave Warsaw at once. She said good-by to her dear father and to her friends and started away to Cracow, the city which had been the capital of ancient Poland. There she knew she would be safe. There she could continue her education and enjoy the privilege of studying Polish literature and history to her heart's content.

After leaving Warsaw, Marie decided to go on to Paris, France, where she could have greater opportunities to study science than could be offered elsewhere. Arriving in Paris, Marie found that her traveling expenses had emptied her purse. No money was left to pay her way through school. A less courageous girl would have given up in despair, but Marie was not easily discouraged. She rented a small back room on the fifth floor of a tenement house and there, with only the most necessary articles

67

of furniture, she set up housekeeping alone. She knew how to keep her living expenses as low as possible. Three times a day— when she ate three meals—she dined on bread and milk, and thus she managed to keep her grocery bill down to ten cents a day. She grew so used to this simple fare that she lost her appetite for meats.

Marie did not like the idea of having to carry all her fuel up four flights of stairs to keep her little room warm during the winter months. Nor did she find much pleasure in doing private tutoring just to earn a few cents to pay her expenses. But since she was determined to study science, she kept up the struggle and sought other part-time tasks where she could earn a little money. Finally she was given the work of caring for the furnace and washing bottles at the Sorbonne.

Whatever Marie undertook, she tried to do well. She was glad to find these new opportunities for work right in the school. Although washing bottles might not be as interesting as making experiments in the laboratory, she did her work thoroughly and in a good-natured manner. Because she performed each simple task assigned her with skill and ease, the headmaster of the physical science department, Gabriel Lippmann, became attracted to her. He saw that this Polish girl was determined to succeed, and he wished to encourage her. He asked Marie about her home life before she came to Paris. Then he wrote a letter to her father, who was still living in Warsaw, and told him what a diligent worker his daughter was. He said also that she would be a promising student in the school of science and that her father might well be proud of her.

While studying in Paris, Marie met another earnest student of science, Pierre Curie, who was one of Lippmann's most brilliant pupils. Like Marie, this young man was poor and struggling through hardships in order to study in the school of science. Day after day, as these young people worked together, a warm friendship developed. They were interested in the same line of work. After a while they fell in love.

Although Pierre Curie had little to offer a wife except his love, Marie Sklodowska married him in 1895, and they lived happily together. They knew how to live cheaply and how to be contented with a simple home. They spent much of their time in the laboratory, and Marie continued her studies at the school. After three years she took the examination for a degree and proved that she was a brilliant scholar.

Marie, now called Madame Curie, began devoting more of her time to the work of science. She became interested in some experiments which other scientists had performed and which she felt should be carried on still further. She set to work at the task and was delighted to find that she was making new discoveries in the world of science. For a while she worked alone without receiving aid from anyone else, but when the work became too great, her husband left his tasks to assist her.

Together they toiled day after day, coming nearer and nearer to the discovery of an unknown element which had baffled scientists for many years. They began their experiments with a ton of ore that the Austrian government had presented to them from its extensive mines in Bohemia. Since they could not handle such a large quantity of material in the laboratory, they began the process of separating it into its different elements in a factory. Then they were able to experiment with the separate elements in the usual manner, returning to the laboratory to carry on this work.

Like all true scientists, Madame Curie was very patient. She continued her experiments for years, believing that someday she would discover the mysterious element which would open up new and greater possibilities to the world of science. Finally she was repaid for her long, hard work, for in 1910 she succeeded in coaxing out of its hiding place in the mineral substance a powerful element which she named radium. Little by little she accomplished this great feat. All the while she had known that the powerful, radioactive substance containing the radium existed somewhere in the minerals, but no scientist had been able to separate it in its pure state. No scientist had even been able to trace it to its hiding place in the mineral.

During the years Madame Curie had worked quietly at her task, but when she made the great discovery known to the world she became famous at once. Noted scientists everywhere sought to make her acquaintance and wished to hear her lecture.

Although her long, hard struggle with poverty now came to an end, Madame Curie had no thought of settling down in luxury and idleness. She continued her experiments for seven years longer before she finally separated the pure radium from the radioactive substance in which it was hidden.

Because of her painstaking labor and skill, Madame Curie was twice honored with the Nobel Prize, the highest mark of distinction that can come to any scientist. She was also appointed chief of the laboratory in the department of science at the Sorbonne, which was especially created for her husband. He, too, had distinguished himself as a scientist and was honored by the school where he had long been a student. After her husband's death Madame Curie succeeded to the position he held in the great school and delivered lectures which were attended by noted persons from all parts of Europe. Her discoveries led to the development of the X-ray and even laid groundwork for atomic energy research.

Madame Curie did not spend all her time at the laboratory making experiments. She also kept house for her husband and two little girls, and during the years of their poverty she solved the servant problem by doing all the work herself. She took time to make her children's clothes and to wash and iron them as carefully as any other mother would. She permitted her little daughters to accompany her to the laboratory, just as she used to go to her father's laboratory.

Although Madame Curie married a Frenchman and made her home in France, she continued to cherish in her heart a love for her native country. She retained her deep interest in its struggle for freedom and rejoiced when the old-new country, after long years of struggling, came again into its own right. Poland, in its turn, feels proud of the fact that it gave birth to such a distinguished woman as Marie Sklodowska Curie.

Chapter 10

DR. WILLIAM GORGAS

Conqueror of Yellow Fever

WHAT terror the news of a fresh outbreak of yellow fever used to bring to the people who lived in the sunny land around the Gulf of Mexico and the Caribbean Sea! Hundreds of them died every year from this plague, and doctors found no way to fight against it. But on the third day of October, 1854, in a fine old mansion near Mobile, Alabama, a baby boy was born, who grew up to fight this strange enemy to the end. His name was William Crawford Gorgas.

William's father was an officer in the United States Army. When a wee little boy, William used to climb onto his father's lap and examine the shining buttons of his uniform. Later he would sit by the hour listening to his father tell of battles he helped to fight in the war with Mexico. "Someday," William used to say to himself, "I will wear a uniform with shining buttons."

Army officers frequently have to move about from place to place, and before William was old enough to start to school his father had served at several army posts. From the sunny South the family moved to an arsenal far up in the New England States, where the long, bleak winters seemed cruel to the little boy who loved to play out of doors in the warm sunshine. Later they returned to the South, living at the army post in Charleston, South Carolina. They were living here when the first guns were fired at the beginning of the Civil War.

William's father became a great general in the Army of the South during this war. He moved his family to the capital, which was first at Montgomery, Alabama, and later at Richmond, Virginia. William used to spend much time with his father at the arsenal. There he met all the great generals of the Southern Army. Sometimes he helped his father by running errands or carrying messages to these men.

Four years is a long time to spend in a war-torn country, and William began to see the dark side of warfare. Soldiers moved about in the streets every day dressed in ragged clothing and without shoes. Often they were hungry and cold. William pitied them greatly and decided to suffer with them. So he refused to wear shoes and ran about barefoot all one winter. In this way he felt that he was becoming a part of the army of heroes whom he admired. Sometimes he went with his mother to carry food to the prisoners, and he helped her carry supplies in her daily visits to the hospitals.

During the war William attended school part of the time, but his schoolbooks did not hold the attraction for him that the military service did. He became a good reader, however, and began to take a special interest in reading the Bible. Again and again his mother found him lying on the floor with the open Bible before him. She felt pleased to think that her young son was learning to love God's Word. She did not know that William's interest in the Bible was confined strictly to that portion which tells about the wars the Israelites waged against their enemies. Old-time warriors, as well as present-day warriors, were interesting characters to this son of a soldier.

One busy day General Gorgas paused long enough to visit the capital and view the body of Stonewall Jackson, which had been brought from the battlefield. He took William with him, and together they looked upon the silent form of a brave man who had given his life for the cause which he believed to be right. William remembered having seen this general at the arsenal, talking with his father. Now he lay cold in death. This experience helped young William to realize more than ever what a cruel thing war is.

One day near the close of the war, news was received that the Army from the North was marching down to seize the city of Richmond. General Gorgas, as a part of the Southern Army, was ordered to leave. No time was allowed for him to move his family to a place of safety. Calling William to him the general issued an order. "Should fire break out near the arsenal," his father said, "be sure to move the family at once to the home of Uncle Thomas. And don't forget to take the cow along."

Soon after his father's departure the city streets filled with troops from the North. Gathering the family together, William started toward his uncle's home, leading the cow by a halter. His mother followed with the baby in her arms and four little girls clinging fearfully to her skirts. They had not gone far when suddenly a terrific explosion shook the ground. Every member of that fleeing group remained calm except the cow; she tore at the halter and ran madly down the street, dragging William by the rope. Presently a bit of flying shell hit her and frightened her still more. With a leap she sprang into the air, knocking William down. By the time he recovered from the shock the cow had vanished. Feeling disgraced at his failure to obey his father's orders, William returned to his mother and sisters.

"It's not so bad, Willie," comforted his mother; "just think —that shell might have hit the baby instead of the cow."

Some time passed before General Gorgas could send for his wife and children to join him in the sunny Southland. For several years they struggled along, sharing the poverty of their fellow countrymen, for times were hard, especially for those who had formerly been accustomed to comfort and luxury.

Better days came when the General accepted an invitation to become president of the University of the South, at Sewanee, Tennessee. Here William could attend college and prepare for the work he would choose to do. These years were happy ones for William.

When his college career drew near to an end, William had to decide what he wished to make of himself as a man. Without a moment's hesitation he expressed his long-felt desire to become a soldier. "Not that, my son," protested his father who had seen so much sorrow in war. But William had decided that no other career would do for him, and so finally his father consented for him to enter West Point. Difficulties now arose which William had not thought of. For instance, he learned he could not qualify for admission to West Point.

Still he refused to be entirely defeated, for he decided that if he could not enter the military service as a soldier he should find some other way to secure entrance. There was a need for army doctors—why not study to become a doctor? The thought pleased him, and he talked with his father about it. In the autumn of

1876 William enrolled as a student at the Bellevue Hospital College in New York city.

In a short time William discovered that he could not have chosen work which he would rather do. No longer was the thought of entering the military service the only motive which led him to his studies; now he studied because he was interested in the work. During those student days he lived so cheaply that sometimes he actually went hungry, and his clothes showed signs of much wear.

After graduating from college William received his first appointment and began his career as Army doctor in the southern states. During his first years of service in Texas he became ill with yellow fever. Fortunately for the world, he had a light attack and recovered fully from it. Thereafter he was no longer troubled with this disease, for persons having it once cannot suffer a second attack. He was now able to care for others suffering from the disease without endangering his own life. Soon he was known as a "yellow fever doctor," which meant that he often had to dig the grave and bury the dead.

Then came the Spanish-American War, and Dr. Gorgas was sent to take charge of a yellow fever camp in Cuba. For many years the capital city, Havana, had been known as a deadly spot because so many people perished there with this strange disease. Now William cared for the sick soldiers in camp and studied the nature of the sickness, trying to find out its cause. But he got no nearer its secret than did other earnest doctors who studied it. They believed the disease to be very contagious and ordered everything used by the diseased to be burned—even the buildings and the doctors' instruments.

One old doctor who lived in Cuba believed that a certain kind of mosquito was responsible for the yellow fever. He insisted that the sting of this insect would cause sickness, but no one listened to him. Dr. Gorgas was sent as chief sanitary officer to clean up Havana when the war ended, and he believed the disease germs thrived in filth. Because the city was very untidy, he and his little army of workmen scrubbed it thoroughly from end to end. They dug ditches and installed a good sewer system. When they had Havana looking very clean and up to date, the yellow fever broke out much worse than it had before.

A company of four doctors now came to Havana and began to experiment with the kind of mosquito which the old doctor had talked about. Very carefully they conducted experiment after experiment. They found the Cuban doctor to be right! The mosquito was the only cause for the strange disease. But what could be done with the mosquito? There were thousands of these insects swarming through the city, especially in and around the buildings. No one knew how to get rid of them. Although the doctors had found out the cause of the fever, they did not know how to kill off the pests.

As chief sanitary officer, Dr. Gorgas learned about the habits of this particular mosquito and set to work with his army of helpers to make war on it. Instead of guns, he and his workmen carried oil cans and poured oil on the surface of all clear standing water, for in such places that kind of mosquito breeds.

Soon the people found out that Dr. Gorgas and his helpers had been successful, for yellow fever cases grew fewer and fewer, until finally there were none at all. Days, weeks, and months passed, and still no new cases were reported. Then everywhere the news spread that William Crawford Gorgas had made Havana a safe place in which to live.

Other places now needed help and Dr. Gorgas was sent to them. First came the Panama, that narrow strip of land through which the French had tried to dig a canal to connect the Atlantic and the Pacific Oceans. After nine years' trying they had given up, for they had dug more graves than anything else. Again Dr. Gorgas went to work. Soon with yellow fever banished and other tropical sicknesses under control, the Panama country became a healthful place in which to live and work. And the United States Government was able to finish the important canal.

Dr. William Gorgas had become famous, but not as the soldier as he had dreamed in his youth. He had done his greatest work, not in caring for sick people, but in preventing well people from getting sick. He had destroyed the cause of one of the most fatal diseases known to mankind. Because of his work he was honored in foreign countries as well as in America. When, on July 3, 1920, he died on a foreign shore someone said of him: "They will take him to his own land, but in truth he belongs to us all. He was one of Life's great helpers, for he cleaned up foul places and made them sweet; and now, as they said of Lincoln, 'He belongs to the Ages.'"

Chapter 11

HELEN KELLER

She Fought Her Way Through Darkness

DAY after day, year after year, a small girl groped her way through the sunny rooms and wide halls of her beautiful southern home. She saw nothing; she heard nothing; she felt deep emotions, which she could not express. No wonder that sometimes she threw herself upon the floor in a fit of rage, crying bitterly because she could not make herself understood. Everywhere was darkness and painful silence; because Helen Keller was deaf and blind.

Little Helen had not always been so. As a baby she had been a normal, healthy, happy child. Born on June 27, 1880, she had for nineteen months grown dearer and dearer to her parents. Then a terrible illness came and it seemed for a while that she would not live. When at last the fever left, baby Helen could neither see nor hear.

Helen's parents took her to many doctors for examination.

Each one said the same thing: This child would never see nor hear again. Finally they brought her back to their beautiful home in Tuscumbia, Alabama, to care for her as tenderly as they knew how. Under their loving care her little body soon regained its strength, but her eyes never again registered light nor her ears sound.

When Helen began to walk she learned to grope her way carefully from one room to another. She learned that there is an indoors and an outdoors. She learned objects by touch, but she did not know that each object had a name. In her dark, silent world she discovered strange things every day, and her wonder grew; for she possessed the natural curiosity of a child who is always asking questions. But she could ask no questions, for she had no language. No wonder that sometimes her restless little mind rebelled in its dark, silent prison!

Even in her dark, silent world Helen found some things which she could enjoy. There were the roses which hung in clusters from the trellis near the porch. She could feel their soft peals, and smell their fragrance. There were the honeysuckles and the jessamine which bloomed in the lovely garden. How she loved these flowers!

As she grew older she wandered about the premises with Belle, the faithful watchdog. Sometimes she followed along with little Martha Washington, the child of the Negro cook, to search for the guinea fowl's nest in the long grass. And when the evening breeze gently fanned her cheeks she felt almost happy.

Helen learned how to amuse herself playing with dolls, much as other little girls do. She could pick out her favorite doll from among the others, and care for it with the affection of a little mother. Sometimes, however, she would vent her displeasure upon it with the cruelty of a tyrant.

One day when Helen was six years old a kind doctor advised her parents to see the famous inventor, Alexander Graham Bell, whose interest in deaf persons led him on to discover the possibility of sending sound over a wire. Dr. Bell urged them to write to the Perkins Institution for the Blind, in Boston, where years before another deaf and blind girl had been educated. Then, with hopeful hearts, Mr. and Mrs. Keller looked forward to the coming of Helen's first teacher.

Miss Sullivan arrived in March, 1887. She brought with her a new rag doll, which Laura Bridgman, the educated deaf and blind girl, had dressed. In Helen's world everybody was kind. And the new teacher was like everybody else. Helen began her lessons without realizing that another world was opening its door to admit her across its threshold. It would be a world of wonder, with meanings which she would understand. It would be a world of words, of names, of books, and of hard study.

Miss Sullivan began by placing the new doll in Helen's arms, and then by slowly spelling the word "d-o-l-l" into her pupil's hand. Over and over she did this, and Helen thought it was great fun. She learned how to spell the letters slowly, just as the teacher had done. She thought it was finger play. She did not understand that "d-o-l-l" spelled a word which was the name of the object she held in her arms.

A month passed by before the meaning of the finger game flashed into Helen's mind. Then one day she stood with her teacher at the pump and felt the cool water run over her hand. Miss Sullivan spelled "w-a-t-e-r" into her hand just as she had spelled "doll." And all at once Helen realized that "w-a-t-e-r" was somehow connected with the cool liquid coming from the pump. A new light came into her face. Now she understood that everything had a name, and she set out eagerly to learn. The ground, the pump, the trellis—three things with which she had been so long familiar, these she pointed to first. And one by one she learned how to spell them, too.

Suddenly she turned to Miss Sullivan, this marvelous person who was leading her across the threshold into a world of meaning, and begged to know her name. "T-e-a-c-h-e-r," slowly spelled Miss Sullivan into the little outstretched hand. Then, with her teacher, she wandered about the place, eagerly asking for names of other things. In a few hours she learned thirty words.

What an excited, happy girl Helen was when she flung herself into her mother's arms that day and made known the fact that she was learning the meaning of things! Every new day meant new words, and soon she was putting words together into short sentences. Now she was playing with slips of cardboard on which were raised letters. These she would arrange together in words. By and by she would put the words together into sentences. All the while she believed she was playing a wonderful game.

At the end of the summer Helen knew more than six hundred words and could use them correctly. There were the puppies and the mother dog in the pump house. There were calves and a colt in the barnyard, and there was a pen full of funny little pigs. Helen could not hear them squeal when Miss Sullivan held them in her arms, but she could feel their squirming little bodies. She remembered the baby chicks which had pecked their way through eggshells while she felt the vibrations with her fingers, and now she asked, "Did baby pig grow in shell?"

By and by Helen learned how to write in raised letters made for the blind, but many of her lessons she still studied outdoors. She learned her first geography lesson down by the river, where she heaped piles of sand for mountains, dug winding waterways and lakes, built dams of pebbles, and had all kinds of fun. Her nature-study lessons she learned in the woods where she examined wild flowers and learned about growing things in the vegetable kingdom. What a patient teacher Miss Sullivan was! And what an eager student was Helen!

When Helen was nearly eight years old, Miss Sullivan believed she was ready to begin studying her lessons in a schoolroom with other children. Then she took her to Boston, to the Perkins Institution for the Blind. Here Helen found little girls and boys who could talk to her in the language of the hand. Also, she found in the library books that were printed in raised type like the letters which Miss Sullivan had taught her to read on slips of cardboard. Soon she was beginning to read these books, one after another, and enjoying every one of them.

When Helen was ready for her first lesson in history, Miss Sullivan took her to Bunker Hill, where she climbed the monument, counting every step. Then she took her for a ride in a steamboat to Plymouth, where she learned about the Pilgrims. Helen was delighted with the ocean, and during vacation she spent many happy hours playing along the beach. One of her first questions there was: "Who put salt in the water?"

As Helen grew older she was not satisfied to speak only with her hands. She knew by feeling the motion of the lips and throat that many people did not use the language of the deaf when expressing their thoughts to each other. She wanted to be able to speak as they did. When she heard of a deaf girl who had learned how to speak she determined to learn too. Miss Sullivan took her to another teacher in Boston, who gave her eleven lessons. These were the most difficult lessons that ten-year-old Helen had yet undertaken, but during the first one she learned six elements of speech, M, P, A, S, T, I. At first she spoke very indistinctly, for she could not hear the sound of her own voice. Often she felt discouraged, but she continued to practice. She talked to everybody and to everything. Her dolls, her books, her pets, and even the birds came in for their share of her conversation. Because of her constant practice and effort to improve, by and by others besides her teachers were able to understand her words.

Then Helen's first thought was to hurry home and speak to her parents. She could hardly wait for the train to stop at the little station in Tuscumbia, where her parents and little sister were waiting to welcome her. The first sentence which she learned to speak was, "I am not dumb now!" Over and over she had repeated those words until she could speak them plainly. What joy her parents and sister had when they heard her speak to them now for the first time!

When Helen was twelve years old she wrote a short story of her life, which was published in the *Youth's Companion.* The following year she visited Niagara Falls and went to the World's Fair. Although she could not see the mighty cataract or hear its roar, she could feel the air vibrate and the earth tremble. At the World's Fair she was permitted to touch the exhibits and to "see them with her fingers." Alexander Graham Bell, who went with her, and Miss Sullivan enjoyed watching her face light up with pleasure as she examined telephones, phonographs, and treasures from all over the world. Perhaps no one at the Fair enjoyed the exhibits any more than did Helen Keller.

The people marveled when they heard that a deaf, dumb, and blind girl had learned how to speak distinctly. They marveled again when, six years later, they heard that she entered the Cambridge School for young women, to prepare herself for college. Already she had studied Latin, French, and German, taking Miss Sullivan to classes to spell the lessons in her hand. She had studied lip reading and voice culture, arithmetic, and physical geography. Now she refused to be satisfied with less than a complete college education, taking the regular courses.

With such remarkable will power Helen was bound to succeed. Miss Sullivan continued to help her where textbooks were not available in raised type, and Helen used her typewriter to prepare the required written work. Thus she struggled through her college years. Sometimes she was discouraged, but she was never ready to quit. In 1904 she graduated from Radcliffe College upon completion of the four-year course. Without the aid of eyes and ears this bravehearted girl had accomplished the same work as had other graduates who could see and hear.

Helen's next ambition was to make herself useful in the world. She thought of the many blind people in her country who have never been trained to become self-supporting. She knew what drab, lonely lives they must live in the dark, with the beautiful things of life shut out from them. She began to urge that they be given an industrial education. She became a member of the Massachusetts Commission for the Blind and served on several advisory boards for the blind and deaf. She wrote books about her experiences and about the educational possibilities of the blind and deaf.

For years Helen Keller lectured before the public in the interests of the blind and deaf. What a marvel it has been to several generations to listen to this woman speak! And what an example of courage and cheerfulness she has been to the rest of the human family, who cannot realize how great have been her struggles through darkness and silence to world-wide fame.

"The Holy Bible has always been my favorite book," Helen replied when being interviewed by a reporter. "I find comfort and guidance in its pages."

Through the work of this great woman thousands of people are able to read these same words of comfort.

Chapter 12

ABRAHAM LINCOLN

"Honest Abe"

ONE morning a proud little boy pulled his coonskin cap down over his tousled hair and started out to follow the trail which led from his home to the one-room log cabin school. Sister Sarah, two years older, led the way, and together they trudged along the forest path over a distance of one and one half miles. Arriving at school they found other boys and girls from other cabin homes, and soon the schoolroom hummed to the merry sound of their voices as they memorized the a-b-c's.

Little Abraham Lincoln had been born in those Kentucky backwoods on a Sunday morning, February 12, 1809. There he spent the first seven years of his life, playing about his cabin door, wading in the creek near by. Sometimes he fished for polliwogs in its sparkling waters, and sometimes he followed his father into the corn patch to help pull weeds. How grown-up he felt on that first morning when he started to school! And how pleased he was to be able to repeat to his mother in the evening what he had learned in the schoolroom that day! He studied his spelling book faithfully, and before the term ended he was able to spell through it and pronounce the words. Soon he would be reading from a book like the older pupils.

And then something happened which interrupted Abe's school attendance for several years. His father decided to leave Kentucky and move into a newer territory. He gathered his few belongings and tied them on pack horses. Then, with his wife and two children, he rode away over the woodland trail leading to the Ohio River. After traveling for several days they came to the wide river, which they crossed in a ferryboat to the Indiana shore.

Although young Abe and Sarah found the new experiences exciting, they were happy when their father told them they had reached the place where he would build their new home. While Abe and Sarah spent many happy hours exploring their new woods and creeks, their father was busy felling the trees with which he built their new shelter. This shelter was called a "half-faced camp," for it was built of logs against the side of a hill. There the Lincoln family spent their first winter in Indiana. Mr. Lincoln made all the furniture for their new home, and this took much time. He also had to clear a piece of ground in time to plant the corn. When all this work was done, he began to build a real cabin home, such as the one they had left in Kentucky.

Only eight families were living in that part of Indiana when the Lincolns came into the settlement, and their homes were far apart. But soon afterward several other families came across the river from Kentucky and settled in the neighborhood. When their cabins were built, the men set to work to build a schoolroom for their children. Abe and Sarah were glad when they could once again enter school. Here, as in Kentucky, all the children studied aloud, and for that reason the school was called a "blab" school. The first book used in this kind of school was a spelling book, and the children were required to spell through the book several times before they began to read. They were also taught how to write and cipher.

When Abe was only nine years old his mother became sick and died. There were no doctors or nurses in the settlement, and several people died from the same illness. Since Abe's father was the only carpenter in the settlement, it became his job to saw out the lumber from the trees and make coffins to bury the dead. It was his sad task to make such a round coffin in which to bury his own wife. No pastor was present to help bury her, but several months later a visiting minister came to the settlement and preached a funeral sermon for all those who had died there.

The year after Abe's mother died, Mr. Lincoln went back to Kentucky for a visit. When he returned to Indiana he brought a new mother for Abe and Sarah. There were also a stepbrother and two stepsisters. This was the beginning of better days for the Lincoln family, and once more the lonely cabin seemed like a real home. The new Mrs. Lincoln was kind to the motherless children, and her three children were fine playmates. No one seemed to mind the fact that the cabin was crowded, for they were pioneers and that was one part of pioneer life.

Young Abe grew very fast. Soon he became a tall, lanky boy, strong enough to help his father clear more land by cutting out the underbrush and chopping down the trees. They then could cultivate the soil and raise more corn to grind into meal for the family use. One autumn Abe worked for days and days clearing a piece of woodland some distance from the cabin.

His little stepsister, Mathilda, begged to go with him, but her mother would not allow her to go so far into the deep woods. One morning she slipped away unnoticed and followed along the trail which Abe took. Presently she saw him up ahead. Thinking she would take him by surprise, she ran quietly behind. When he stopped she sprang forward and ran into his sharp ax, which cut a gash in her ankle. Abe bound up the wound with cloth which he tore from his shirt. When she had stopped crying, he asked, "Tilda, what are you going to tell Mother about getting hurt?"

"I'll tell her I did it with the ax," she answered, hanging her head. "That will be the truth, won't it?"

"Yes, Tilda, that's the truth, but not the whole truth. Tell the whole truth," he urged, "and trust your good mother for the rest."

Nearly all the people who lived near Abe in his youthful days were uneducated, and the whole of his schooling was less than a year. But during this time he became a good reader, and books held a strange charm for him. Because the Lincolns were poor, they had few books in their home. Young Abe had to borrow books from his friends to read. Those that he read and reread during his boyhood were, first of all, the Bible, then *Pilgrim's Progress, Aesop's Fables, Robinson Crusoe,* Weem's *Life of Washington,* and a history of the United States. Often he would sprawl on the floor in front of the open fireplace during the long winter evenings and read by the light of the blazing pine knots.

When Abe grew up to manhood his father decided to move again into a newer country. This time he loaded his family and some of their belongings into a big prairie schooner, hitched two yoke of oxen to it, and turned westward toward Illinois. A slow, tedious journey that was—over frozen ground, thawing roads, and partly frozen streams. Abe drove the oxen much of the distance. One day when they had forded an ice-coated stream they found that their pet dog had been left behind. Looking back, they saw him jumping about in great distress. He did not want to be left behind, and yet he dreaded to plunge into the icy water. The family did not want to forsake him, but still they could not afford to waste the time recrossing the stream just to recover a dog. So they decided to move on. This was too much for Abe. Pulling off his boots and socks, and rolling up his trousers, he waded into the chilly water and triumphantly returned with the shivering little animal tucked under his arm.

After a journey of two weeks the travelers reached the Sangamon River, about ten miles west of Decatur, Illinois, where they decided to build a new home. Abe and his stepbrother helped Mr. Lincoln cut down trees to build the cabin. Then they helped him clear ten acres of land and plant a field of corn. When this was done they split rails to make a fence around their field, and during that time Abe was kept too busy to do much reading. Day after day he swung his ax and split the logs into rail lengths; then he helped to build the fence.

Across the river from the new Lincoln home lived a neighbor who wished to build a fence around his land also. Hearing that Abe was a rail splitter, he came one day and hired him to help split thousands of rails for him. The wage he offered was small, but Abe was glad to earn a little money, so he took the job. At another time he split rails to pay for a suit of clothes. He had to split four hundred rails for every yard of homespun cloth used to make the clothes.

But Abe was not content to be a rail splitter all his life. He wanted to do something useful for his country and the world. In 1832, when the war with the Black Hawk Indians was being fought, he enlisted as a soldier and was lected captain of the military company from his neighborhood.

River navigation was an important means of transportation during those days, and Abe hired out as a riverman on a boat going down the Ohio and Mississippi to New Orleans. He made two trips down the river on flatboats that carried produce to the South. Here he saw for the first time the evils of slavery. The sight of human beings chained together like beasts in groups to be sold at the market made him feel greatly troubled. He saw slaves put on the auction block where they were sold to the highest bidder. He saw the terror on their faces as they felt the rough hand of their new master. With a sad heart he turned away. "If ever I have a chance," thought this tall, sober-faced youth, "I will do my best to end the slave business." Years later it was he who, as president of the United States, issued the Emancipation Proclamation, which set all the slaves free.

Abe did not work long as a riverman, because he believed he could find more important work to do. He spent several years working first at one thing, then another; then he became interested in law and politics and decided to become a lawyer. But he knew that lawyers are educated men, and he had no education. This did not discourage him greatly, for he borrowed books of law from a friend and set to work to study them carefully. He entered politics and was chosen by the people of his district to be their representative in the state legislature. This work took him to the state capital, where he met educated men and women. All the while he continued to learn by studying books and observing people, until he became a prominent man in Illinois politics.

Still Abe kept on reading and studying and learning about the needs of his country. He learned about the wrongs that were threatening to destroy the nation, and he longed to help right them. It was not long until the United States of America needed such a man as Abraham Lincoln for its president. His countrymen believed they could trust this honest, humble man to make wise decisions for the good of all the people. On the fourth of March, 1861, he took the oath of office and became president of the United States.

Only a few weeks after Abraham Lincoln became president, his country was plunged into one of the bloodiest wars of its history. The people of the North and the people of the South fought against each other. This war brought much sorrow to the President, but never once did he give up hope of reuniting the states under one flag. So strong was his faith in this united nation that during the war he declared the freedom of the slaves who lived in the South. When the war ended, the slaveholders gave the Negroes their freedom.

Near the close of the war Abraham Lincoln was re-elected to serve a second term of four years as leader of the nation. Only a few weeks after his second term of office began he was shot and killed by a man whom many persons believed to be mentally ill.

Abraham Lincoln will always be remembered for his honesty, his concern for the rights of all people, and for the humble way he lived and worked. This is only a brief part of the story of the boy whose life began in a lonely cabin back in the hills of Kentucky and ended in the nation's capital, where he served in the highest office of his country.

Chapter 13

JENNY LIND

"The Swedish Nightingale"

A LITTLE Swedish girl sat near the window in her grandmother's room in Stockholm one day, singing to her pet cat. She had sat by the same window doing the very same thing many times before. Quite often she had seen people who were hurrying along the street below stop suddenly and stare at her in wonder. She did not understand why they should stare so. Her kitty never stared when she sang. She only curled up like a furry ball, purred contentedly and blinked her eyes until she fell asleep.

One of the listeners on this particular day chanced to be a servant girl of Mademoiselle Lundberg. She stopped, stared, and listened, just as other people had done. Then she hurried home to her mistress and told what she had seen and heard. "No child ever lived who had a sweeter voice," she declared emphatically. Mademoiselle Lundberg was deeply interested. She was a prominent woman who loved music. "I must hear the child for myself," she said.

Jenny Lind, who came to be called the "Swedish Nightingale," was the child singer of our story. She had been born in Stockholm on October 6, 1820. The first three years of her life she spent in a small village ten miles from the city. Then, because her hard-working mother was not always able to provide a home for her, Jenny sometimes stayed with her grandmother in Stockholm.

It was the grandmother who first discovered that Jenny possessed unusual musical talent. She made the discovery in this way: A square piano stood in her best room, and one day not long after three-year-old Jenny came to stay awhile with her she heard somebody playing a tune on the instrument. She had forbidden the child to strum on the piano, thinking her scarcely more than a baby. Jenny's elder half sister sometimes practiced her music lessons on the piano, and now the grandmother supposed that it must be she who was picking out a melody with one finger instead of doing her lesson properly. So she called to her from the next room, but received no answer. Wondering at the strangeness, she went into the room to investigate and was surprised to find no one. Before leaving the room, however, she stooped down and looked under the piano. There, crouched on the floor, lay her little granddaughter Jenny.

"Child, was that you?" the astonished woman asked as she drew the little one from her hiding place. Jenny, sobbing out her story on her grandmother's knee, answered, "I heard the buglers playing in the streets and I wanted to play the tune myself. I did not mean to be naughty."

"Don't cry, child," soothed her grandmother. "It is I who did the wrong. Hereafter you may play whenever you hear a tune in your mind."

Not long afterwards Jenny's mother came to the city to see her children, and the grandmother told her of this incident. "Mark my word," she said, "this child will bring you help someday."

Much as Jenny was delighted with her success in coaxing melodies from the keys of her grandmother's piano, she enjoyed singing still more. From morning until night as she skipped about her play she sang. Indoors and out of doors her childish voice rang clear and sweet. Sometimes the neighbors came in to hear her play. But the music of her singing might be heard at any hour of the day. As she grew older they often shook their heads and said, "Too bad that nothing is being done to train that child's remarkable voice."

Jenny's grandmother was a Christian. Often she talked to the little girl about the heavenly Father. She told her that her wonderful talent for music was a gift from God. All through her lifetime Jenny believed that her grandmother was right. She tried to use the wonderful gift God had given her just as she believed he wanted her to use it.

When Jenny grew old enough to enter school she returned to her mother, who was then teaching. For several years she enjoyed the privilege of having her mother with her at home and in the schoolroom, too. She studied her lessons thoroughly and was a bright pupil.

The time came when Jenny's mother could no longer earn enough money teaching school to pay expenses. So she sought other employment and sent the child back to live again with her grandmother in Stockholm. At first Jenny must have felt lonely in the city, and so she whiled away the hours singing to her pet cat. And that is how she happened to be singing when the servant girl saw and heard her through the window.

Not many days afterwards Jenny's mother received a note

from Mademoiselle Lundberg: "Will you please bring your little girl to sing for me?" the note read. This was Jenny's first invitation to sing before someone capable of judging musical talent, and how eager she was to go! The fact that she would be singing to a wide-awake, critical lady instead of to a sleepy cat did not make one bit of difference. Dressed in her Sunday frock, she went with her mother to the lady's apartment at the appointed hour.

And how she did sing! The lady sat listening in amazement, tears trickling down her cheeks.

"Wonderful!" she exclaimed, when the song was ended. Then turning to Jenny's mother, she said, "Your child is a genius indeed. You must have her educated for the stage."

"Not for the stage," came the quiet reply, for, like her grandmother, Jenny's mother feared that the influence of stage life would be harmful to her little daughter.

"Then at any rate she should be taught singing by the best instructor," the Mademoiselle insisted.

For a long time Jenny's mother had wished to give her a musical education, but she could not afford this. She explained how impossible this had been, and the kind lady replied, "Perhaps we may find some other way." She then asked permission to write a note of introduction to her friend, Herr Croelius, the court secretary and singing master of the Royal Theater. "Take this to him," she said; "it may lead to something."

Jenny's eyes grew wide with anticipation as they bade their new friend good-by and turned their footsteps toward the opera house. She was going to see a singing master! And perhaps he would ask her to sing for him as the Mademoiselle had done. She wondered whether he, too, would like her singing.

When they reached the studio and presented the note of introduction, they met the gentleman and chatted for a while with him. He asked questions about his little visitor, and by and by he brought a sheet of music and asked her please to sing for him. Jenny glanced at the music and saw that it was familiar. Then she sang her very best. When she finished the song she saw big tears rolling down the cheeks of her astonished listener.

"I must take her at once to Count Puke, the head of the Royal Theater," said he to Jenny's mother, "and tell him what a treasure I have found."

But the busy count did not receive his visitors as graciously as had the singing master. When he saw the shy, plain-faced little girl standing before him he did not look pleased. He asked her age, and upon hearing that she was nine years old he said impatiently, "This is not a nursery; this is the King's school."

"Very well," replied Herr Croelius, turning away in disappointment, "if you refuse to hear her now I shall teach her myself, and someday she will astonish you."

The count was surprised at these words flung at him so bitterly from the singing master. He glanced a second time at the shy plain-faced little visitor about to leave the room. "Stay," he called, "and let me investigate the matter further."

It had been easy to sing for the Mademoiselle, who had invited Jenny to her apartment. It had been a joy to sing for Herr Croelius, the kind singing master. But when this critical, stern, great man asked her to sing for him, that was quite a different matter. However, Jenny resolved again to try to do her best. She sang with all her heart, and the count stared at her in wonder, just as the listeners had often stared at her from the streets below her grandmother's window. She did not mind that he stared, for she saw his hard face soften. He had been convinced, just like the Mademoiselle and Herr Croelius, that little Jenny Lind was no ordinary child.

Now the count was very eager to enroll Jenny as a pupil of

the King's school. He proposed that she be adopted into the school of pupils attached to the Royal Theater. Thus all her expenses would be paid and she would receive the very best training. At first her mother felt unwilling to consent to this arrangement, but finally she agreed, and Jenny Lind's musical education began.

For eleven years Jenny drilled at the Royal Theater. She believed that although God had given her a talent for music he expected her to improve it as much as possible and that was her reason for studying so faithfully. During this time she lived in an apartment near the Royal Theater, where her mother kept several other pupils as boarders. In this manner she was permitted to be with her mother every day, and she resolved never to allow the influence of the theater to spoil her life. She admired the beautiful Christian character of her mother and of her grandmother, and she determined to become a good woman as well as a great singer.

By and by Jenny Lind began to make concert tours through Sweden. Wherever she went she thrilled the hearts of her listeners, but she felt that she was not yet prepared to do her best. She wanted to continue her studies in Paris under a master artist, so she saved the money which she earned from these concert tours to pay her expenses in Paris.

No student was ever more determined to succeed than was this Swedish maiden. When she arrived in Paris she found out that she had nearly lost her voice. Instead of giving way to discouragement she set to work in earnest to study the French language, and at the end of three months she was able to go on with her music lessons. Now she studied under a noted master in Paris for ten months. She received some benefit from his teaching, but she declared that she sang after no one's method. She loved to watch the birds sing, and she approved of their method, which she felt had been taught to them by the Master of all creation.

The first concert which Jenny Lind gave outside of her native Sweden was in Copenhagen, where she had gone to visit friends. She had not intended to sing in public while there, but was urged to do so by Hans Christian Andersen, the renowned writer of *Fairy Tales,* and his friend, A. A. Boumonville. The concert which she gave was such a success that her fame soon spread all over Europe.

Words of praise did not turn Jenny's head. She went just as willingly into the humble room of a sick man to sing for him when he could not go to the concert to hear her as she went to her most successful concert. She tried just as hard to please one listener as thousands.

With the coming of fame, Jenny entered upon a busier life than she had known before. Because of the invitations which came from all over Europe and from across the sea to give concerts to music-loving people, she traveled from one country to another, singing her way into the hearts of her listeners wherever she went. In her own country she was treated like an empress. Thousands of people lined the streets to see her pass through her home city, Stockholm, when on her way to England. Even the warships in the harbor were decorated for the occasion, and all fired salutes, just as they did when the king himself was being honored.

When Jenny Lind sang at court before the royalties of Europe, she showed the same naturalness and simplicity which marked her singing elsewhere. She attended the receptions given by members of the royal family in her honor, and entered into the social life of the fashionable people. But she remained the same unspoiled singer who first won the applause of the people.

At the beginning of her career as a singer Jenny Lind sometimes disappointed her audience when she first appeared on the stage. She was then a thin, shy, plain-featured girl, somewhat nervous and awkward. But when she rose to sing her face and form seemed to undergo a change, just as if the grace and purity of her soul were shining through. No one who saw and heard her sing said that she was plain. They felt that they were listening to the voice of an artist who cherished in her heart a reverence for God.

The vast sums of money which Jenny Lind received from her concerts she did not use selfishly. It is said that no woman ever gave away such wealth from her own earnings as this singer did. In America alone her earnings amounted to about one quarter of a million dollars. Much of this she gave away at once, and the remainder she reserved as a charity fund to be distributed after her death. She gave the receipts of many of her public entertainments to charity, and in her native country she founded a school in which the poorest girls could receive an education. She urged the cultivation of art and character in this school, especially of character.

For nearly half a century Jenny Lind's wonderful voice thrilled the hearts of audiences wherever she sang. She lived to see her grandchildren cluster about her knee while she told them about the loving Father-God whom her own dear grandmother had introduced her to when she was a little child. Then, when the last days on earth approached and she was confined to her bed, she thought longingly about the time so soon to come when she would be singing again, forever free from pain. One day when the window blinds had been opened to let in the sunlight, she raised herself on her pillow and sang a song she loved—"Und dann Sonnenschein" ("And Then Sunshine"). Soon afterwards her happy spirit went to the place where eternal sunlight never fades and songs of gladness never end.

Chapter 14

DWIGHT L. MOODY

Salesman for God

ONE November evening two boys wandered down the main street of a New England village and stopped in front of a hardware store to look at the display in the window. The younger of them, a little fellow only eight years old, had been crying. In spite of his brother's efforts to interest him in some attractive object in the window, Dwight continued to sniffle. What did he care about jackknives or marbles or baseballs when he was lonely and homesick?

Earlier in the day the two boys had left their home and walked thirteen miles to this city where they would live during the winter and attend school. Here they could earn their board and room by doing chores and running errands. But Dwight had never been so far from home before, nor had he ever been quite so unhappy.

Just then an old man came tottering down the street toward them, and Dwight's brother said, "Here comes a man who will give you a penny."

"How do you know?" asked Dwight, doubtfully.

"Because I've been here before, and I have seen him give a penny to every new boy who comes to town."

That sounded reasonable, so Dwight made a brave effort to hide his tears, and walked into the middle of the sidewalk where the old man would be sure to see him. When the man approached he stopped and said, "This is a new boy in town, isn't it?"

"Yes, sir," replied Dwight's brother, politely. "He just came today."

Dwight expected to see him put his hand into his pocket at once and take out a penny, but instead of doing that the old man took off Dwight's cap and placed his hand on the small boy's head. He talked to the boys and learned why they had come to the village. Then he looked into Dwight's tear-washed eyes and told him about the heavenly Father who loved him. Dwight felt that the old man loved him, too, for he listened quietly to his quavering voice, almost forgetting about the penny he had expected. Presently the stranger reached into his pocket and took out a brand-new penny that looked just like gold and gave it to him.

To Dwight that small penny seemed like a fortune. His father had died when Dwight was only a four-year-old, and his mother had needed every penny to feed and clothe her family of seven boys and two girls. No wonder he treasured that cent! Long after the treasure was spent, Dwight remembered the kind words with which the old man had eased his heartache that day.

Dwight's father had died suddenly, leaving many debts and no money with which to pay them. Even the home in which the family lived was mortgaged, but the law of the State preserved it for the widow and her children. Soon the creditors came and took everything they could carry away—even the kindling wood. The next morning the children had to stay in bed until time to go to school, for there was no way to warm the house. That very morning Dwight's Uncle Cyrus came to their rescue by bringing a load of wood and cutting it into stove lengths. More than once that kindhearted man helped the struggling family. Neighbors predicted that Mrs. Moody could never keep her family together to rear them to respectable manhood and womanhood. Years later when Mrs. Moody died in that same community, she had convinced every doubter that a good mother is not a quitter.

Dwight, her fifth child, was born on her birthday, February 5, 1837. Dwight and his brothers and sisters were fun-loving, home-loving children. Although the older boys hired out to farmers near their home town of Northfield, Massachusetts, during the summer months, they always came home on Saturday evenings to spend Sunday with their mother, brothers, and sisters. Thus Mrs. Moody kept the family together one day out of seven while the boys and girls were growing up.

Sundays were never-to-be-forgotten days for the Moody family. With sunset on Saturday evening a quiet reverence settled over the home and lingered until sunset on the following day. The family were regular in attending Sunday school and church services. The boys used to go barefoot, carrying their shoes and stockings in their hands until they came in sight of the church. Then they stopped to put them on.

After Dwight grew to manhood he often praised his mother for having so faithfully helped her children form the habit of going to church. For a time, when he could not understand the minister's sermons, he used to feel peeved because he had to go to church. But later when he grew up and went away from home, he found that the habit had become so fixed he did not care to break it.

Dwight's first experience as a wage earner came when one summer he took the neighbor's cows out to pasture on a mountain. He received one cent a day for his labor. When eight years old he hired out with an older brother to cut broomcorn for a farmer who lived across the river from their home. More often he hired out during the winter months to do chores and earn his board and room while going to school.

A stern, quick-tempered schoolmaster took most of the joy out of the schooling that Dwight received; for, unfortunately for Dwight, his love of learning did not always keep pace with his love of fun, and as a consequence he received numerous floggings. When a new teacher—a woman—came into the schoolroom, the boys expected to have a gay time. And Dwight, their leader, felt sure that his days of suffering from whippings the teacher gave him were at an end. The new teacher had announced that she expected to rule the school by love!

When on the first morning she opened the day's lessons with prayer, a hush fell over the scholars. They had never seen the like of that, and felt awed and quieted. After several days the newness began to wear off, and Dwight found himself the first violator of the schoolroom rules. When the new teacher requested him to remain after school he stiffened himself, expecting the usual fate. Much to his surprise, she did not attempt to punish him. Instead, she sat down beside him and talked quietly about the way he had been behaving. He soon felt ashamed, and promised to obey the rules. Never again did he disappoint her by causing trouble in the schoolroom.

One lesson that Mrs. Moody taught her children was the importance of keeping a promise. When once they agreed to do a certain thing, she held them to it. She never asked, "Can you do it?" but rather, "Did you say that you would?" One winter Dwight had agreed to work for a neighbor for board while attending school; but after spending some time there he came home complaining that for nineteen meals his only food had been corn meal and milk with occasional pieces of bread too hard for the family to eat. His mother asked if enough food was set before him to satisfy his hunger, and when she learned that he had plenty to eat, such as it was, she sent him back to keep his agreement. Dwight learned to be very careful about making promises!

At the age of seventeen Dwight Moody went to Boston to find work. He had an uncle living in that city whom he hoped would offer him a place in his shoe store, but no job was offered. After searching elsewhere and finding no one willing to hire him, he came to his uncle one day and asked for work. His uncle feared that Dwight might not become a successful salesman, but wished to encourage him. So he told him that he would hire him if he would promise to take advice and to attend Sunday school and church services regularly. This Dwight promised to do, and in a short time he surprised his uncle by becoming the best salesman in his business.

Dwight had not been in Boston long when one day the man who taught his class at Sunday school came into the store to talk to him about becoming a Christian. As a result of that talk Dwight was persuaded to give his heart to God.

While still a very young man Dwight left Boston and went to Chicago to find work. He hoped to make a great deal of money and someday become a very rich man. Here he worked again in a shoe store and continued to be a salesman. He worked faithfully, and his employer quickly learned that Dwight was a Christian and could be trusted. Soon others learned that Dwight was busy every waking moment. On Sundays he attended church, taking with him the young men whom he could persuade to leave the streets and go into a house of worship. At the church he rented four pews, which he planned to fill with young men who did not attend services anywhere.

One Sunday afternoon Dwight visited a mission Sunday school where the poorer people attended services. He told the superintendent that he would like to teach a class, but the superintendent replied that already he had more persons wishing to be teachers than pupils to be taught. "If you will bring scholars for a class, you may teach," the superintendent said. The next Sunday Dwight returned with eighteen ragged boys whom he had gathered from the streets. He did not keep the class for himself, but volunteered to go out and find other scholars, and soon there was a thriving Sunday school.

Not long afterwards Dwight visited another part of Chicago where there were no churches, but many saloons and gambling places. He decided that would be the very place to begin a Sunday school, and so he rented a hall. He began to gather in the neglected children who had never been taught about the love of God. His Sunday school grew until the place was filled, and then the school was moved into a larger building. The enrollment reached one thousand. Although many of the children were rough and ragged when Dwight first brought them into his Sunday school, some of them grew up to be respectable citizens of whom Chicago felt proud.

The only attraction Dwight Moody used to get new pupils for his Sunday school was kindness. Many of the children came from homes where there were drunken fathers and mothers and where kindness was unknown. Dwight visited such homes and persuaded many of the parents to become Christians. His Sunday school grew into a community church, and Dwight grew into a preacher!

Not long afterwards the world began to hear about this earnest young preacher, and Dwight L. Moody was invited to other great cities of America to hold revivals. He crossed the Atlantic Ocean to Great Britain twice to conduct evangelistic campaigns in the British Isles. Wherever he went thousands of people flocked to hear him. Always he remained the same humble, earnest Christian man who started his work for God in the slums of Chicago.

For more than forty years Dwight L. Moody worked for God. He returned to his home near Northfield, Massachusetts, in 1899, where he lived until God said his work was done.

Chapter 15

IGNACE JAN PADEREWSKI

Genius at the Piano

IN THE garden spot of Russia—Podolia—there once lived a gentleman farmer and his wife whom the outside world came to hear about through their son, Ignace Jan Paderewski. This son was born to them on November 6, 1860. Little did they realize when they wrote his name on the family register that someday the world would honor him because of his remarkable skill as a musician.

Like all babies of all time, he cooed and cried, ate and slept, and grew until he began to "get into things." Time and again, to keep him out of mischief his mother held him on her lap while she sat at the piano playing beautiful melodies. Wide-eyed with wonder and delight, he watched her fingers glide smoothly and nimbly over the keys. Besides watching the fingers as though spellbound, he liked the sound of the musical tones which came from the instrument.

As a baby Ignace and his small sister shared in the love their mother poured out on them. What happy hours they spent together! The days, weeks, and months passed in that quiet country home, and Ignace grew into a fine little boy.

Then one day a great sorrow entered the Paderewski home, for the mother became very ill and at last died. Another sorrow followed. Cruel soldiers came to the home, seized the father, and dragged him away to a cold, bleak land called Siberia. There he was forced to work like a slave. Because he was suspected of being unfriendly toward the Russian government, these soldiers had taken him from his home and children to a land of strangers and hardship.

Little three-year-old Ignace and his sisters were left like orphans. Kind people cared for them, giving them a home with plenty of food to eat, warm clothes to wear, and a soft bed in which to sleep. But there was no mother to listen to their evening prayers and to tuck them snugly into bed. There was no kind father near to try to comfort them when they felt unhapppy and to praise them when they did their best.

In spite of these sorrows little Ignace continued to grow straight and taller every year. After several years had passed by, news came that his father was returning from the land of exile, a free man. Eagerly, the children watched at the gate for his arrival. They threw themselves into his open arms with joy when the wonderful day came.

Through tears Mr. Paderewski looked into the faces of his son and daughter and realized that they were safe and well. He saw, too, that they had grown in mind and body and that now they should be getting acquainted with schoolbooks. "My children must have a good education," he said, and he began to plan how he might engage the best teachers for them.

One day he saw Ignace sitting at the piano his mother had

loved to play. A simple little melody of his own composition kept running through Ignace's head. "Listen to my tune, Father," he called.

His father was pleased with what he heard. "I will do my best to give you a musical education," he said as he praised his son for his composition. Soon arrangements were made with an old teacher to visit the homestead once a month and instruct his children how to play the piano.

So few and far between were those early music lessons that Ignace could not advance rapidly. Yet he found plenty of time to practice each lesson well before the teacher came to hear him play. He also found time to compose little melodies for his own entertainment. "I must study hard, practice well, and learn everything that I possibly can about music, so I can give the very best kind of music to the world." With this determination he continued his studies at home until his twelfth year, when his father arranged for his further education in the city.

Warsaw, the capital of Poland, was the city to which his father sent him to school. There Ignace was able to have regular music lessons at the Warsaw Conservatory, with the best teachers his country could offer. However much the twelve-year-old boy missed the freedom and quiet of the country, he did not complain. Now he would work as hard as he could to become a great musician. True, there were other subjects besides music to be mastered, for in order to become a great composer he would need to understand the longings and the needs of his fellow men. He studied other languages and learned from reading their books what the people of other nations think and feel and desire. But always he returned with the greatest enthusiasm to his study of music and to his practice at the piano.

After spending four years in school at Warsaw, Ignace began to give public concerts. From one place to another he went throughout the country, playing his own compositions before the audiences. During this first tour he came to a small town where he had announced a concert and found that there was no piano in the hall where the concert would be given. Of course, he could not play without a piano, and so the search began. Was there anybody in the town whose instrument they might hire for the night? No, that was not the question—was there anybody in the town who had a piano? Only one piano could be found in the whole town. This one was badly out of tune and the hammers refused to return to the keys after they had been struck. What should be done? The crowd was beginning to assemble in the audience room, and the youthful musician had to think quickly.

"Bring the old piano over," he ordered, "and we shall see what we can do."

While several men were bringing the piano another hurried away to bring a whip, and then a strange experiment took place. Ignace struck the chords, and an attendant struck the stubborn hammers with the whip when they refused to come down. And, wonder of wonders, it worked! So the unusual concert began, and "Bang!" went the chords, and "Swish!" went the whip, much to the amusement and entertainment of the entire audience.

Ignace was then only sixteen. When he finished that tour, he felt he should return to Warsaw to resume his studies before attempting to give more concerts. He enrolled again at the conservatory as a student of the piano and continued his studies until he was eighteen. Then he was appointed professor of music at the conservatory.

At first the appointment pleased him, for he was still very young and did not realize that teaching music might be tiresome work. But when day after day passed by, with pupils coming for instruction from morning to night, Ignace grew restless. He had little time to call his own and no time to continue his studies. Instead of enjoying his work he began to dread it. At the end of the term he gave up teaching in Warsaw and went to Germany.

In Berlin, Ignace studied composition with two capable teachers, for he still longed to compose music for others to play. Then he consented to accept another appointment as pianoforte teacher at the Strassburg Conservatory. During his few years there he met a celebrated actress from his homeland who took an interest in his artistic career. She urged him to continue his studies and prepare to give concerts, for she believed that he possessed rare talent as a musician. "The world will applaud you as a genius of the finest type," she said.

Ignace yielded to her persuasion and went to Vienna to study under a famous teacher for nearly four more years. He was already an accomplished musician, but he realized that if he hoped to do his very best he must do better tomorrow than he did today. At the end of his first year in Vienna he appeared in concert and was greatly applauded. He refused to allow this degree of success already attained to become his greatest, for he continued to study longer.

Then, after long, hard years of study and work, Ignace at last started out to let the world of music lovers hear him play. First he went to Paris, where the French music lovers received him questioningly, wondering whether he could please. But when they heard him they were thrilled, and for the entire season they enjoyed his concerts.

Soon the English music lovers in London heard about the famous young artist who had charmed Paris with his skill at the piano, and they began to wonder whether, after all, he was as wonderful as he had been advertised. Ignace Paderewski did not leave them wondering long, for he went to London at his first opportunity. And the English music lovers, like the French music lovers, found out that he was indeed deserving of their greatest praise.

By this time the new pianist had become famous in Europe, for both the French and English people appreciated him greatly. Now he looked out across the broad Atlantic Ocean and thought of the music lovers in America. They, too, must have an opportunity to hear him. So he bade his European friends good-by and sailed for New York.

Music lovers in America were wondering whether he deserved all the praise which Paris and London had given him. They came to hear him for the first time, not at all sure about this European. But they went away satisfied, for they had been convinced that he belonged to them just as much as he belonged to the Old World. He showed that he understood the longings of music-loving people everywhere.

On his first visit to America, Ignace Paderewski stayed six months and gave 117 recitals. So greatly was he appreciated that he was urged to return the next season and play again for the American people. His second visit was even more successful than the first. Everywhere he went crowds gathered to hear him. Special trains were run from neighboring cities to carry the people who could not otherwise attend his concerts. In Texas whole schools marched many miles to hear him. Sometimes crowds would line the streets from his hotel to the concert hall just to get a glimpse of this famous man.

Visiting artists often find tours of America very exhausting. Going from city to city, lodging in one hotel and then another, is very wearing on the nerves of sensitive artists. Ignace Paderewski preferred to travel in a private railway car. Here he had his own regular cook who prepared his meals at the hours he wished to eat. In the observation room of the car was a piano, for he still felt the need of practice in order to do his best. When preparing for a recital tour he seldom practiced less than ten hours a day, and then he would often lie awake at night thinking about each part of the program.

Ignace Paderewski's greatest ambition was not to become a famous pianist, but rather to compose musical numbers for famous artists to play. Nevertheless, he found himself listed among the most famous pianists the world has known.

Chapter 16

LOUIS PASTEUR

He Thought Things Through

EVERY bottle of pasteurized milk left at our doorsteps is a silent reminder of the great man, Louis Pasteur, who gave his life to make the world a healthier, happier place.

The birthplace of this great man was a humble dwelling in the quiet village of Dole, France, not far from the Swiss border. His parents were called peasant folk in France. They were plain, humble people. His father had once served in the army of France under Napoleon. When Mr. Pasteur laid aside his sword to build a home, he engaged in the tanning trade to make a living. He married the daughter of a market gardener who lived near the tannery, and Louis was their first child.

Like all parents, the Pasteurs believed their child was a wonderful lad and they wanted to give him a chance to grow up into a wonderful man. They believed he should have a good education, and although they were poor they began to plan for this before he was old enough to enter school.

Not far from Dole was another town, Arbois, where a tannery was located. In this town was a very good school, just the kind suited to the needs of a lad like Louis. The Pasteur family moved to Arbois in order that Louis might enjoy the privileges of this school. Already they had taught him the alphabet, for his father could hardly wait until Louis might learn to read. Using the French a-b-c's, they had taught him how to spell words for them to pronounce when he was just a wee boy.

In the primary room of the Arbois school Louis soon felt at home among a group of students who spelled words aloud in a sort of singsong. The teacher divided the group and appointed one in each group to instruct the younger members. Although Louis was the youngest member in his group, he wished very much to become the one chosen to teach the others. He studied his lessons so well that soon he was able to recite without making a mistake. It did not take him long to become a leader in his school.

Louis was a thoughtful student. He always wanted to be very sure that he understood his lessons before going on to new ones. Because of his unwillingness to rush ahead the teachers considered him slow, but his father was pleased. "Louis will understand every page he turns," said his father proudly. Every evening in the Pasteur home found Louis and his father bending over the lessons and reviewing past work. In this way Mr. Pasteur had an opportunity to study also. As a little boy he had been denied the opportunity to go to school, and now he was glad to be a student with his son.

When Louis was not in school he liked to play about in the tannery yard. What great fun he and his chums found in dodging about among the pits that had been dug in the yard for the preparation of skins for tanning! Sometimes he and his friends would go down to the river near by and catch fish.

At the age of fifteen Louis was ready to enter a school of learning higher than the college of Arbois. One of his instructors, the headmaster of Arbois school, had been urging him to study to become a professor. Often they had walked about the grounds together, and Louis had listened with sparkling eyes while the headmaster told of the bright future which might await him if only he would continue his studies in Paris.

Louis' father was too poor to send him to school in Paris. Besides, he felt unwilling to part with his son. He wondered how he could live without having Louis near by. Then he remembered that someday Louis would be a man, ready to do a man's work, and he knew it would be unwise for him to refuse to let the boy continue his education and prepare for a useful life. When friends offered to help with the expenses of Louis' schooling in Paris, Mr. Pasteur consented for him to go.

Never afterwards could Louis forget that bleak October morning when he told his parents and little sisters good-by and set out on the tedious journey to Paris. He had to travel in a crowded stagecoach to the nation's capital with only one school companion to accompany him. Neither of the boys had been so far from home before, and both of them felt lonely and unhappy. But the miles passed one by one and after the last change of horses, the coach came swiftly into Paris.

"Here," thought Louis, "I will study so hard that I will be able to forget my longings to be at home." But try as he might, he could not overcome his homesickness. He could not eat; he could not sleep except to dream of home; and he could not study as he had studied when attending the school at Arbois. Everything was strange and new, and he could not accustom himself to the change. "If I could only get a whiff of the tannery yard," he told his friend one day, "I feel that I should be all right again." But there was no tannery yard near by. When several weeks passed, his instructor grew uneasy lest Louis should become really ill and sent word to the boy's parents.

Not many days later someone called to Louis and said, "They are waiting for you close by." Not knowing whom to expect, he went to the place indicated and there found a man sitting at a small table in the back of the shop, his bowed head in his hands. With one look at the stooped form of the man, Louis recognized his father. With a glad cry he greeted his parent, feeling sure that his father had come for him.

Sure enough, Mr. Pasteur had been just as unhappy because of the separation as Louis had been. The two journeyed back to the village home, and Louis decided to study to become an artist instead of a professor. Already he had shown an unusual talent for drawing, and this seemed to be the kind of work for which he was best suited. He enrolled once more at the Arbois school and set to work in earnest with his paints. In a short time he advanced so far that his instructor could teach him no more. Yet he could not become even a successful artist without receiving more education!

Once more the kind headmaster talked to Louis about his future work. "Art is good," he said, "but I feel that you could do better than become an artist. Try again to continue your other studies, for surely you can now succeed."

Not long afterwards Louis enrolled in a college not far from his home town, where his father frequently went to buy and sell skins. He knew the visits of his father would help keep up his courage; besides, he was now growing old enough to realize that someday he would have to go on without his father's help.

In the new school Louis took a keen interest in his studies. He liked to experiment with chemicals, and one day he performed his first scientific experiment by extracting phosphorus from bones. Later on, when he became a professor, he encouraged his pupils to prove by experiment in the schoolroom what they learned from textbooks.

Before Louis could actually begin his work as a professor, he needed to take some training in Paris. He returned the second time to that city and entered school. No longer did he suffer from homesickness, for he had decided to prepare himself to teach science and he knew that he must study hard and long in order to do that. Often he wrote long letters to his parents and sisters telling about his life in Paris and about the experiments he was making in the classroom.

One day after Louis had been experimenting for a long time he made a discovery which drew the attention of noted scientists from other countries. In those days many people believed that such creatures as lizards, flies, and bees mysteriously grew out of thin air. Louis knew that they must be mistaken. "No living thing can come from empty nothing," he insisted. Then he set about to prove by his experiments that such a belief is only superstition. In doing so he did discover that the air contains millions of tiny living organisms called germs, which cannot be seen without the help of a microscope. He proved that these germs often cause the worst diseases among people and animals. He experimented very carefully to prove these facts. Then he found a way to prevent much of the suffering and death from cruel diseases that were formerly spread by these tiny germs.

The people of France began to realize that Louis Pasteur was a great man. When disease threatened to destroy their cattle or sheep they sent for him to come and find out what caused the disease and what could prevent it from spreading among their flocks and herds.

One day a call came from the southern part of France. This

time Pasteur was wanted to save the people in a stricken district from poverty. They depended on the silkworm industry for a living, and their silkworms were dying by the hundreds. Some strange disease which they could not understand was threatening to ruin their business. Louis had never studied worms and knew nothing of their habits, but he answered the call from those distressed people and went to see if he could help them. First he had to study the silkworm, and then he learned what was causing the disease. For many months he experimented before he was able to learn the right thing to do. "He has saved our country from financial ruin," said the king and queen of France. "He deserves great honor and respect."

As Louis Pasteur grew older he thought more about helping suffering people. He discovered the method of heating milk to the temperature where germs are killed. This process, which became known as pasteurization, has been responsible for saving the lives of people throughout the whole world.

One disease whose mysterious cause haunted Pasteur was hydrophobia. No one had ever found a successful way to treat this terrible illness. Every person or animal affected with it suffered the worst agony, and there seemed to be no cure. Louis decided to find a cure. He first studied the disease by experimenting with rabbits and dogs which had hydrophobia. After making many tests he discovered a way to prevent animals that were bitten from getting sick and dying. Then he wanted to see if the experiment would work with people as well as with animals. Fearing this might be a dangerous experiment, he thought he would not endanger the life of anyone else, but experiment on himself. He intended to allow himself to be bitten and then to subject himself to the same method of cure which had been successful in treating bitten animals. Before he had time to do this a call suddenly came to him to treat a nine-year-old boy who had been severely torn by a mad dog on his way to school. The boy's parents had heard about the success of Louis' experiments with bitten animals, and they believed that he could save the life of their child. Rushing him to Paris, they begged Louis to cure their son. "But the cure has not been proved on people," Louis informed them. "It is our only hope," the parents answered. "Without your help he cannot live. We will take the chance if you will accept his case."

Louis Pasteur could not turn these parents and their sick boy away. "I will do what I can," he promised them, and he set to work. Several weeks' time was required in order to complete the cure, and during this time Louis learned much about this dreadful disease. At the end of the time of treatment the boy was cured and was able to return home.

This was a great triumph for Louis. Afterwards he was called to treat other persons who had been bitten by rabid wolves or by other mad animals. Some people came even from other countries to receive his treatment and be cured.

Louis Pasteur lived to be seventy-two years old, and until the end of his useful life he kept busy studying how to help other people. He received the highest honors from the rulers of many countries. But fame did not change him, for he always remained the same quiet, earnest, energetic man, ready to help wherever he was needed.

Chapter 17

MARY SLESSOR

The First Woman Missionary

OH, I wish I could help the bush children," sighed a little Scotch lassie one day after hearing her mother tell about the boys and girls in faraway Africa. "I am going to be a missionary when I grow up and go out there and teach."

"But you're only a girl," protested her brother. "I'm going to be the missionary from this house." Then seeing how disappointed his remarks had made his sister, he added in a generous tone, "It'll be perfectly all right for you to come and help me, though, if you're real good. I'll let you sit up in the pulpit right beside me."

The two young daydreamers were Robert and Mary Slessor, children of a shoemaker who lived in Aberdeen, Scotland, about the middle of the nineteenth century. Their mother was a Christian woman, deeply interested in missionary work. She hoped that at least one of her children would someday help to tell the Christian story to people in a faraway land. When she heard the talk of these two little ones she smiled, and in her heart she prayed that if it pleased God her little Robert might indeed become such a man as he now aspired to be. But God chose to call Robert to himself not long afterwards.

Now Mary became the eldest child in the family, and a very dependable child was she. There were few toys in the plain home, but Mary found enjoyment playing with her baby brother and sisters. She could care for them and dress them and hush them to sleep like a little mother. Sometimes when the younger children did not need her care she would play at teaching school. All alone in a corner of the room she would sit, talking to the imaginary children in her schoolroom. Her mother, overhearing her remarks, would know that Mary was still thinking about helping the bush children in faraway Africa.

Although Mary's mother was a Christian, her father was not. He kept company with men who drank wine and whisky and seemed not to care what it did to them. As a result, he himself began to spend most of his earnings for drink. Often on Saturday nights he would come home with his pockets empty and his mind clouded by whisky. When drunk he was often cruel to the family and the children would rush out of doors to hide until he would go to sleep.

In his better moods Mary's father was ashamed of his weakness, and he decided to move away from Aberdeen, leaving his old friends in hope that he might get away from the temptation to drink. He left his shop in the city and moved his family to the busy, smoky town of Dundee, on the River Tay. Here there were many large mills and factories, and the streets climbed right over the tops of steep hills overlooking the countryside. Sometimes Mary would take the children for long walks, and they would climb the hilltops and gaze on the green fields lying along the river. Sometimes when the tide came in they would go down to the riverbank to breathe the fresh smell of the sea.

But Mary's father did not leave his bad habits behind when he moved away from Aberdeen. Soon he was drinking as before, and his wife was forced to go to work in one of the mills in order to buy food and clothes for the children. Now Mary was left to do the housework and care for the little ones. She did not mind these tasks, but she did mind the sadness which her father's conduct brought their home.

By the time Mary was eleven years old her father had become a hopeless drunkard, and her mother could not always earn enough money to provide for the family needs. There was no law against child labor in those days, and so Mary took her place among the other children who worked long hours in the factory. At first she was allowed to work only half a day. The other half she was sent to school at the factory, where the working girls were taught to read and write and count.

Mary was glad for the privilege of going to school. She was eager to learn how to read and write, but she did not like numbers. They seemed to dance before her eyes and get themselves all mixed up as she tried to work simple problems on the blackboard. Long years afterwards when she taught the bush children in Africa she felt sorry for the ones who were dull in mathematics. She remembered how confusing the numbers used to look to her when she was a child, and she was patient with her pupils.

Although Mary found her arithmetic lessons hard to learn, she was clever with her fingers and soon knew all about weaving. Then her name was placed on the pay roll at the factory and she became a wage earner. How pleased she felt when she ran home with her first week's earnings! She laid the money in her mother's lap and danced up and down with happiness. To her surprise, she saw tears roll down her mother's cheeks. It hurt her mother to take the money young Mary brought home. She felt children should not be required to work in this way.

In a few years Mary was working at a large machine and receiving good wages. She spent long, tiresome hours at her work, waking each morning when the factory whistles blew at five o'clock. She took her place in the factory, ready to begin the day's work, at six. She would keep the machine going until six o'clock in the evening, having only two hours off for lunch periods during the day. In summer she often carried her lunch and ate it in the factory. Then she would go out for a walk in the park, to get away from the noise of buzzing machines and whirling belts.

Saturday afternoons and Sundays Mary did not work in the factory. She always found plenty to do at home to help her tired mother get ready for Sunday, and when Sunday came she took her brother and sisters to Sunday school. Mary always studied her Bible lessons carefully, and the teacher always knew that Mary would be able to answer the questions correctly. When she was quite young she became a Christian and there came into her heart a great desire to learn more and more about Jesus and his loving ways.

As Mary grew, her longing to become a missionary kept growing, too! But she knew that now her mother hoped to educate her brother John for the ministry. "John will be our missionary, now that Robert has gone to heaven," she had often heard her mother say. Mary understood how much her mother needed her earnings at the factory, for she was the wage earner for the family now. She worked on quietly and asked God to help her find some work to do for him at home.

The church Mary attended was built over shops and looked down on streets which were filled at night with big boys and girls who had no Christian training. They were rude and wicked, and Mary longed to interest them in better ways of living. But they refused to attend church and pretended to care nothing about God. Soon a mission was opened on a side street, and Mary believed that these young people might be persuaded to attend services there. She asked the superintendent of the mission if she might have a class in his school. She looked so small and frail that the superintendent feared the work would be too hard for her. He knew the young people would be difficult to work with. But when he saw the eager longing in Mary's eyes he consented to let her try.

Mary had no easy time trying to start her class. The young people insisted that they did not want anybody to bother about them, and many refused to come. Some who attended were rowdy and hard to manage. Gangs would gather outside the building and throw stones and mud against the walls, trying to frighten the Christian workers. Mary refused to be discouraged. Although she suffered unkind treatment she never acted frightened or angry. When they saw she was no coward, they quit bothering her. They even began to follow her to the mission to take their places in her class. They soon grew very fond of their teachers and tried in awkward ways to help in the work she was doing.

Feeling that she needed to know more about the young people in her class, Mary visited in their homes. She found that they lived in wretched places, but she paid no attention to untidiness and filth. She talked with their mothers, took the dirty babies on her knees, and acted so friendly and willing to help that soon she won her way into the hearts of these people. They were ready to listen to her teachings, and some of them tried to do better.

During these years Mary's brother John grew tall, but he was a frail lad. The doctor finally said that John could not live much longer in the cold climate of Scotland. They sent him to New Zealand, hoping the change would do him good, but soon after arriving there he died. His mother's fond hopes of a missionary son were never fulfilled.

One day while Mary was grieving over the loss of her brother, the thought flashed into her mind that now, after all, she would have to be the missionary from that family. Both Robert and John were gone, and there were no more boys for her mother to offer to God. Now the missionary would have to be a daughter. The thought came again and again, "Perhaps you are the one whom God has chosen to carry the story of Jesus to the bush children in Africa."

Mary knew she was uneducated, but she could not stop her work to go to school. She knew, too, that her mother depended on her, and she wondered how the family could get along if she should leave them. But she believed that if God really wanted her to go as a missionary he would help her find a way. She began to study harder than ever. She would borrow good books, or buy them, and slip one into her pocket to take to work. Often she propped a book open on a corner of the loom, where she could read a few lines whenever she had a minute to spare.

Though she studied whenever she could, Mary never slighted her work. She was one of the cleverest weavers at the factory, and by working fast she found that she could increase her pay check. Each week she laid aside more money in a savings account for the needs of the family if she should go away. On Sundays she took advantage of opportunities to speak in public services until she learned how to put her thoughts together in clear and simple words.

Days, weeks, months, and years passed while Mary was preparing to become a missionary. For fourteen years she toiled as a factory worker, working hard and waiting patiently for her call to a foreign land. Then one day the sad news came to Scotland that Dr. David Livingstone, the great missionary hero, had died in Africa. "Send another volunteer to take up the work he left undone," came the call from that faraway country. Mary felt that God wanted her to answer that call.

Mary's mother was glad to give her daughter to work for God in Africa. "You'll make a fine missionary," she said, "and I'm sure God will be with you." Then it was easy for Mary to leave her loved ones and sail away.

At first Mary went to Calabar, not far inland on the west coast of Africa. Efik is the principal language used in that part of the continent, and Mary's first task was to learn it. She studied hard, and in a short time was able to converse with the natives. This surprised her fellow teachers and pleased the natives. They said of her that she was "blessed with an Efik mouth." Then her old, old dream came true, for she began to teach boys and girls in the day school.

Mary loved every one of the children and was disappointed because there were so few in her school. She found out that the African chiefs did not believe in educating children and that was the reason why only a few came to be taught. At first she laughed to see the children carry their slates on their heads and their pencils in their woolly hair. She found that some of them were mischievous, fun-loving children, just the same as the boys and girls in her own homeland. Sometimes she went out to the primitive "yards" where they lived and talked to their fathers and mothers about the love of Jesus.

At first Africa seemed like a wonderland to Mary. She had spent so many of her waking hours shut up within factory walls that now her eyes feasted on the forest green and the beautiful scenes. Though there was much beauty to see, Mary also saw the terrible conditions under which the people lived and she longed to do whatever she could to help these people.

Mary spent several years at the first station in Calabar, getting acquainted with Africa's people and their need. Then she went to another station farther up the river. Here she lived in a hut built of mud and slips of bamboo, with a roof of palm leaves— a "sure-enough" African house. She wore old clothes and ate cheap food. In this way she saved some of her salary, which she sent back to her widowed mother in Scotland. The natives respected her ways and were pleased to have her live among them. By and by they listened to her when she objected to their wicked customs, and some of them began to do better.

One of the evil practices of the Africans which grieved Mary was the killing of twin babies. Her mother had told her stories about this evil practice. Now she saw that the Africans were really afraid of twins. She resolved to show them how foolish their superstition was. One day she found a twin baby that had been thrown away into the bush to die. A little black baby girl it was, and she named it Janie. The natives looked on in horror and would not come near the child. They expected something dreadful to happen to Mary because she took the twin. But nothing happened. Whenever she heard of twin babies who had been thrown away she hurried out to find them.

Mary often talked to the grownups about the "Jesus way." They would gather in groups about her and listen very closely while she explained to them the words of God. They began to call her "the Ma who loves babies." Sometimes they called her Ma *Akamba,* which means "The Great Ma." By and by they respected her so much that even grown men and women began to mind her like children.

When the natives started to quit their evil ways and try to worship the true God, Mary sent for other missionaries to come to teach them. Then she gathered her few belongings together, packed them into boxes, and piled them into a boat on the river. Taking the children, she rowed upstream into another district where the story of Jesus had never been told. Here she built another African house and set up housekeeping, and little by little she won the respect and confidence and love of her new neighbors. Over and over Mary endured the hardships of such beginnings, sometimes going into districts where she did not receive a welcome. "We do not want to change our ways; we do not want your teaching," the chiefs would say, frowning at her. But Mary stayed!

She had such a strong influence over the natives that the British government appointed her consul of the district in which she lived. Dr. Livingstone had held this same government position while he toiled in Africa, but Mary was the first woman to be thus honored by Great Britain. She refused to wear the blue cap with a gold band that showed she was a British consul. "It is enough," she would say, "that the natives know and that they respect my decisions in court."

Mary spent thirty-four years of hard work as a missionary. Many of her friends in that land called her "The White Queen," but the natives called her by the more endearing term of "Our Mother." Many of the boys and girls whom she saved from cruel death in the bush grew up into Christian men and women who loved and cared for her when she became old. The fact that she had been the first woman missionary did not impress them; but the beauty of her Christian life had won them to God and the Christian way.

BOOKER T. WASHINGTON

Slave Boy and Educator

HUDDLED together on a pallet of rags that had been spread on the clay floor in a corner of the cabin, lay two little boys asleep. The younger of them stirred, opened his eyes and looked about. Something had awakened him. Through the dim shadows he saw the kneeling form of Mammy Jane, her face uplifted in prayer. What was she saying? Little Booker listened, and this is what he heard: "Dear God," prayed Mammy Jane, "here I is an' my chil'ern, jes' slaves. Look on us with pity and give us freedom, dear God, please give us freedom!" As Mammy Jane prayed, little Booker grew wide awake. What could it be that Mammy was wanting so very, very much? He was too young to understand the dreadful meaning of slavery, but from that moment he realized that whatever it meant, he and his mother and brother were slaves.

On the large plantation where little Booker lived were many other slaves. Mammy Jane, his mother, cooked for the master and his family, also for some of the slaves who worked in the fields. Long hours she spent every day preparing food for them, and little time was left to care for her own growing family. How she longed to see the day come when she might walk out that cabin door a free woman, leading her children into a free country.

The plantation on which Booker was born was in Franklin County, Virginia, several miles from a small station called Hale Ford. The date of his birth is not known, but he was only a small child when the terrible war broke out between the North and the South which called so many white men away from their homes to fight. During those years he remained with his mother on the plantation. He grew from carefree childhood into boyhood just like the other children on the plantations, often having little food and less clothes. These days of war were full of trouble for both the white and black people.

One morning in the springtime a messenger came to Mammy Jane's cabin door and told her that she and the children were wanted at the "big house." All the other cabins on the plantation were also visited by the messenger, and every slave was asked to appear at the same place. They gladly dropped their work and marched in whispering groups to the master's house. They knew very well what this summons meant, for although none of them could read they had somehow kept informed about the happenings in the outside world. They had learned that the great man Lincoln had proclaimed their freedom. Still they had pretended not to know, and until the war closed they had gone about their daily work as usual. Now the white men had returned from battle and the slaves were told that a new life would begin for them.

Sometime before the war ended Mammy Jane's husband had gone away to West Virginia to find work in the salt furnaces. Now he sent a wagon to bring his wife and her children to live with him. This was the first time Booker had left the plantation, and the outside world seemed wonderful to him. The trip was a long, hard one, for the road led across the rough mountains and food was scarce. The children walked much of the distance, sleeping at night in the wagon or on the ground. After many days of travel they arrived at the little shanty in West Virginia where they began their new life.

Although Booker could not have been more than eight or nine years old, his stepfather soon obtained work for him and his older brother in the salt furnaces. One day he saw a young man reading a newspaper to a group of listeners, and he, too, edged his way into the circle to listen. How wonderful it would be if he could read. But Mammy Jane could not teach him, for she had never handled a book in her life. Neither could her husband, for he did not know how to read. Booker made up his mind that somehow or other he must learn, and he told his mother of his great desire.

About this time a gentleman who came into the neighborhood opened a school for colored children. Mammy Jane got a book for her son, hoping to start him with the other children, but her husband felt that Booker could not be spared from his work. So a disappointed little boy, hiding his tears as best he could, trudged on to the salt furnaces, while his more fortunate playmates learned their a-b-c's in school. "Never mind, Honey," comforted his mother. "You'll learn someday."

Day after day Booker had seen barrels of salt packed in the mines and marked with certain letters. By watching these closely and by asking questions he learned the letters, and before very long he could read as well as some of the children who went to school. Then after a while his stepfather consented to let him go to school half a day if he would get up early in the morning and work as much as possible before schooltime. This he did willingly, rising so early that he was off to work at four o'clock in order to quit in time to be at school by nine o'clock.

Although Booker's first day in school was the happiest day of his life, it brought a strange embarrassment to him. He noticed that when the teacher called the roll every child had two names. He had only one. He quickly decided to choose a second name for himself. When the teacher asked for his full name he replied, "Booker Washington."

One Sunday morning as Booker and some other boys were playing marbles in the road an old man passed by on his way to Sunday school. He stopped and talked to the boys, telling them that they ought to go to Sunday school too. Until this time Booker had never heard of a Sunday school, but he grew so interested in the old man's description of the school that he put his marbles into his pocket and started to Sunday school that very morning. Thereafter he attended regularly, and when he grew older he taught one of the classes. When he became a young man, he was superintendent of the Sunday school.

Booker's first school days did not last long, for the family was so poor it made it necessary for him to spend whole days at work. About this time his stepfather sent him to work in the coal mines. What a horror came into his heart when for the first time he entered the dark, damp shaft that led far back into the mountain! He took his book along, and in spare moments he tried to read by the light of the little lamp which hung on his cap. Not long afterwards his mother hired someone to teach him at night. But this new teacher was poorly educated and unable to teach Booker very much.

Mammy Jane, however, was not discouraged. She kept looking about, and she found a place where her son could work as houseboy. His new employer was a woman, and at first Booker thought she was very strict. He had never been taught the necessity of neatness, cleanliness, and order; for his own mother, having had no opportunity to learn these things, could not teach them to her children. She urged him to learn all that he could from this good woman, and after a few discouraging experiences Booker began to appreciate his new employer.

While in her employ he continued to take time to study, sometimes attending school in the afternoons, and the rest of the time engaging a teacher at night.

After spending four years as houseboy, Booker decided to go to the Hampton Institute, in Virginia, to continue his education. He had heard that in this school poor students were given an opportunity to work for their board.

The first task assigned to Booker at the Hampton Institute was that of sweeping a classroom. How thankful he was then for the careful training he had received under his strict employer when he worked as houseboy! Now he knew how to sweep and dust as well as a trained janitor; so he did his very best. The principal of the Institute was so well pleased with Booker's work that she said, "I think we will try you as a student." He continued to do his best work, and in three years' time he graduated with the regular class.

Because his older brother had helped to pay his expenses, Booker decided that now he should earn money to help pay his brother's way through the Hampton Institute. He returned to his home town and began to teach school. For three years he continued there as a teacher, in both day and night school, besides conducting two Sunday schools on Sunday. Then he spent another year in study at the Wayland Seminary, in Washington. Just what work he was preparing himself for, he had not yet decided; but he knew that in order to be his best in any place he should secure as good an education as possible. For a time he thought of becoming a lawyer. After a while he felt sure that he could do more good in the world as an educator of his people, and so he gave up his study of law.

From this time Booker thought a great deal about the problem of helping his people. Less than twenty years had passed since he, a little, ignorant, ex-slave boy, had marched with them into the land of freedom. He saw that millions of them were still ignorant and poor. They needed someone to teach them how to help themselves become useful citizens of the great country they loved so dearly. And he decided to do his very best to help as many of them as he could. Then one day a call came from the South for an educated man to organize a normal school for Negro students, and Booker Washington answered that call.

At Tuskegee, Alabama, Booker found a group of people who wished to establish a school at that place in which to train educational leaders for the Negro people. He listened to their plans and encouraged them to go ahead. They appointed him principal of the normal school and opened summer school in an old church building and a little shanty that was almost ready to fall down. These buildings they gladly furnished as best they could with necessary school equipment, and on July 4, 1881, Booker Washington began his great lifework as an educator of his people.

From this humble beginning the Tuskegee Normal and Industrial Institute grew under the leadership of Booker T. Washington into the greatest training center for Negro students in the South. Here the yearly enrollment, after numbering thirty students that first summer term, grew into thousands of young men and women who came from all parts of the South to fit themselves as teachers and trained workmen.

Booker Washington's remarkable ability as an educator and his unselfish devotion to his lifework won for him many lasting friendships among the best citizens in the world. He was welcomed by kings and queens of Europe during his vacation abroad, and everywhere he was treated with the greatest respect. Accomplished as an orator, he was invited to address audiences of thousands of people. Always in simple words he spoke the longing of his heart to help his fellow men become honest, respectable, worth-while citizens.

After spending thirty-four years in ceaseless work, Booker Washington's tired body wore out, and he was laid to rest beneath the sunny skies of the Southland that he loved so well. The great work which he began is still going on as a living monument to this truly great man.

Chapter 19

THE WRIGHT BROTHERS

Two Boys Who Did What Couldn't Be Done

FOR long, long years people had been thinking, "Would it not be wonderful if we could soar in the air like birds?" They had been saying, "If God intended for men to fly, he would have given them wings."

But every now and then someone happened along who wanted to learn how to fly. "We have minds capable of thinking and planning and discovering things unknown to us before," those persons said, "and we might be able to make wings with which to fly." They would try and try and try again, and just as often they would fail to discover the secret of flying. Other people laughed at them for spending their time foolishly trying to do what couldn't be done! Someone wrote an amusing story about "Darius Green and His Flying Machine," and people who read the story supposed that only simple-minded persons, called "half-wits," would try such ridiculous stunts as learning how to fly.

No one enjoys being laughed at and called a simpleton. But now and then somebody who possesses the needed courage dares to try to do what he believes can be done, and trying again and again he proves by and by that he is right. The world owes much to the bravery of such intelligent men who will keep right on studying and experimenting until they succeed in the inventions they have set out to make. Listed among such courageous men we find the names of Wilbur and Orville Wright, inventors of the airplane.

These two brothers were the sons of a minister, Bishop Milton Wright. Wilbur, the elder, was born near Millville, Indiana, on April 16, 1867, and four years later, August 19, 1871, Orville was born in Dayton, Ohio.

Although Bishop Wright was a busy man, he took time to think about the needs of his growing children. He remembered how it felt to be a boy, and when he saw interesting toys in the shopwindows he knew his sons would be delighted to play with them. Sometimes he would step inside the shop and ask the clerk to wrap up a certain toy which particularly attracted his attention and which he believed his boys would appreciate. Just one toy would be enough for the two boys, for they played well together.

One evening the bishop came home with a bulging package tucked beneath his arm. Wilbur, then eleven years old, and Orville, seven, were so occupied with their play that they did not see him unwrap the package. They scarcely heard him enter the room; but when he said, "Here's something for you, boys!" they glanced up to see a strange object dart through the air and bump against the ceiling, then fall to the floor.

"What is it?" they cried, as they ran to pick it up.

"Scientists call it a helicopter," explained their father.

"Let's call it a 'bat,' " suggested one of the boys, and to this the other one agreed. Their other game forgotten, they now gave full attention to the maneuvers of the "bat." Again and again they picked the crumpled toy from the carpet, twisted the rubber bands tightly, and hurled it through the air. And just as often they laughed to see it buzz about overhead, bump against the wall or ceiling, and fall limply to the floor. What fun they did have with that "bat"! Presently the rubber bands snapped, and then the delicate, paper-covered wings could fly no more. The fun was over and the broken "bat" was tossed aside.

One day, when the boys were older, they decided to build another "bat" like the one their father had bought at the shop. They made a light frame similar to the cork-and-bamboo frame of their broken toy and covered it with paper. Then they took two rubber bands and adjusted them so that when they were tightly twisted they would drive the paper-covered wings in opposite directions. When all was ready they threw the home-made toy into the air and it flew just as the shop toy had flown. They had built their first flying machine!

"We'll make a bigger one now," they decided, after watching the first one fly about. But they learned that a bigger "bat" could not fly so well as a smaller one. "Something is wrong," they agreed, "but what is it?" Since neither of them could find out, they grew tired of making small "bats," and decided to manufacture kites instead.

Building kites seemed better sport than building "bats," for kites can fly high above the treetops and do not bump into the sky. Sometimes the strings tangle in the telegraph wires and sometimes they break and let the kite fly away; but on the whole, Wilbur and Orville had much fun playing with their kites. While watching them glide upward and soar about overhead, the boys used to think how much fun it would be to make a kite big enough to carry a man.

Of course, the Wright brothers did not spend all their time at play. They attended school in Dayton and took an interest in their studies, for they found out that schoolbooks answer some of the questions of why and how that they had often asked each other. As they grew older they began to read other books and magazines.

Orville decided that he would like to enter the printing business, and so he built a printing press and began to print a boy's paper called the *Midget*. He succeeded so well that he bought a better outfit and began to print a weekly newspaper called *The West Side News*. Wilbur became the editor of the paper and Orville remained the publisher.

Just as kite-flying had once been their favorite out-of-door sport, now bicycle riding became their favored hobby. They became expert riders on their bicycles and entered various races.

They took pride in keeping their wheels in good condition and did their own repair work. After a while they grew more interested in bicycles than in the printing business. So they opened a shop where they built and repaired bicycles. While engaged in this business they studied mechanics carefully and learned how to make improvements on their bicycles. Every bit of work that passed through their hands was well done, for they were painstaking workmen. Building bicycles was just as much fun to them as building "bats" had been. And always their customers were well pleased with the work done in the Wright brothers' repair shop.

The years passed by and Wilbur and Orville grew to manhood, working together just as happily as they had played together. One day in the autumn of 1896 they read in the newspaper an account of the death of a German inventor who had been trying to learn how to fly. This man had built wing-like devices called "gliders," and with these he had made more than two thousand glides through the air. Then while experimenting in this manner he had lost his life.

The Wright brothers had never forgotten their boyhood interest in building flying toys. They remembered how they used to build kites stronger and better than any of their friends could build. They knew that their love for flying kites had been so strong they might have continued the sport all through the years had they not grown too big to play with the kite-flying boys of the town. The flying apparatus had been put away in order to take up other interests more like those of other young men their age.

Now as they worked together in their bicycle shop they talked the matter over and decided to take up kite manufacturing again.

"People will laugh at us and call us fools," they said; "but we will let them laugh. This time we will build a kite strong enough to carry a passenger."

They set to work to build something like a box kite. Then they tried to fly this machine in a strong wind. Each of them made daring experiments while trying to ride in the great kite, but they had to admit failure. Their machine needed more power than the wind supplied to lift it from the earth with a passenger in it.

Now the brothers realized that they needed to understand more about the air and about engineering. Neither of them had attended college, but both of them set to work to study and learn all that they could from books and magazines. As they studied they experimented to find out whether the book knowledge was workable. Whenever they found it was at fault they kept on experimenting until they learned the right thing to do. For several years they studied and worked, until they had no more money with which to experiment.

The people who used to have business dealings with the Wright brothers shook their heads and said it was a pity that those fine young fellows had lost their heads over trying to make a silly invention. They did not believe people would care to risk their lives flying, even if someone should discover how the trick could be done.

There was one person living in Dayton who believed Wilbur and Orville Wright were on the track of a great invention. That person was their sister Katherine. She was teaching school and earning a small salary, a part of which she willingly lent to help her brothers. With this money they were able to go on with their work until they invented the airplane.

For a time the brothers worked and experimented near their home in Dayton, but after several years they decided to go to a different place and carry on their experiments undisturbed by onlookers. They went to a lonely spot in North Carolina, called Kitty Hawk, and built a rude shed for a workshop. There they spent several more years building machines with which to experiment, and all the time learning more and more about the mysteries of flying. At last, on December 17, 1903, they actually flew. What a long time they had spent learning how to balance their machine, how to build an engine that would lift it off the earth and force it through the air, and how to guide it in its flight! With these things learned, they had discovered a secret that mankind had never known before—the art of flying.

Still they needed to improve their machine much before it would be ready to make long flights. They needed to spend several more years patiently working and paying no attention to the unkind remarks which thoughtless people would make about them. This they did, and at last the time came when they knew they were ready to give public performances.

Wilbur went to France in 1908, and there he successfully demonstrated his ability to control his plane while in the air. The following year he gave public demonstrations before the king of Spain, the king of England, and the king of Italy. He convinced them that he had mastered the long-sought art of flying. At home Orville was giving public performances with his plane, and soon the Wright brothers found themselves the most talked-about men in the world.

After they had succeeded in building machines that could fly, Wilbur and Orville worked just as hard trying to improve them. They continued to work together and to study the problems of flight until May 30, 1912, when Wilbur died of typhoid fever. Then Orville pursued his studies alone. Later he became chief engineer of the Wright Aeronautical Company and director of its laboratory at Dayton, Ohio.

Because of the patience, determination, and skill of these brothers the world now possesses the most rapid means of transportation known in the history of man. Where formerly weeks, days, and months were required to cross continents and oceans, now these distances can be spanned by planes in hours by the clock. Less than twenty-five years after the first plane lifted itself into the air, brave young adventurers, such as Colonel Charles Lindberg, made nonstop flights across the Atlantic from America to France; and Commander Richard E. Byrd took his plane over the dangerous ice of the North Pole. By that time airplanes were being used to carry passengers and mail across the country, to aid in map making, forest protection, exploration, and advertising. Every plane that flies in any part of the world carries the same means of control which was first invented by Wilbur and Orville Wright.